W9-AVJ-774

Cookin' Up

COUNTRY
BREAKFASTS

GET SET TO SERVE UP SOME MMM-MEMORABLE MORNINGS!

IN THE COUNTRY, households begin bustling with activity *before* the break of day...even in the kitchen. There are always early-morning chores that need doing—and hungry families look forward to "refueling" with a delicious hearty breakfast afterward!

So among "breakfast experts", no one knows more than country cooks. And, in *Cookin' Up Country Breakfasts*, they're sharing their *very best* breakfast dishes with *you*.

Thanks to this colorful, easy-to-use, photo-filled cookbook, you now have the recipes for *hundreds* of unbeatable family-favorite breakfasts right at your fingertips. All of them are filling, flavorful and truly different. What's more, all of them can be made with ingredients you likely already have right on hand—a big bonus for any busy cook.

Wait until you see your family's faces light up when you first serve them Mary Bitterman's morning-mealtime specialty, which she appropriately calls "My Husband's Favorite Omelet" (recipe on page 27). Mary, who's from Willow Street, Pennsylvania, says that during more than 40 years of marriage, her husband has asked her to make that omelet for him *at least* once a week!

Or how about Carol Trotter's "All-in-One Egg Casserole" (recipe on page 14)? It's a combination of eggs, bacon, cheese, vegetables and bread all cooked up in one pan that's been drawing her raves for years in her Inman, South Carolina kitchen.

Plus, in addition to those and many, *many* more Skillet Specialties and Oven Dishes, this big book brings you plenty of recipes for Pancakes, Waffles & French Toast, Magnificent Muffins, Breads & Spreads and Satisfying Cereals, along with ideas for Fruits & Beverages and even Breakfasts for Kids.

So *relax*. Everything you need to escape the "What would they like for breakfast *this* morning" jam is right in your hands!

Editor: Julie Schnittka
Food Editor: Mary Beth Jung
Assistant Food Editor: Coleen Martin
Test Kitchen Home Economists: Karla Spies, Rochelle Schmidt
Test Kitchen Assistants: Judith Scholovich, Sherry Smalley
Assistant Editor: Kristine Krueger
Art Directors: Linda Dzik, Stephanie Marchese, Ellen Lloyd
Photography: Scott Anderson
Illustrations: Jim Sibilski

©1994, Reiman Publications, L.P.
5400 S. 60th St., Greendale WI 53129
International Standard Book Number: 0-89821-190-5
Library of Congress Catalog Card Number: 94-61367
All rights reserved.
Printed in U.S.A.

TABLE OF CONTENTS

PICTURED ON OUR COVER. Clockwise from the bottom: Farmhouse Omelet, Meal in a Muffin Pan and Bacon and Eggs Brunch (all recipes are on page 5).

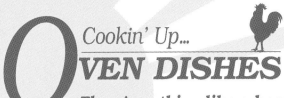

Cookin' Up...

OVEN DISHES

There's nothing like a hearty fresh-from-the-oven breakfast to get a family's day off on the right foot—and these favorites from all around the country fit that bill warmly and flavorfully!

FARMHOUSE OMELET

Frances Drake, Woodbridge, Virginia
(PICTURED AT LEFT)

When my children were growing up, weekend breakfasts were full of surprises because the refrigerator was full of leftovers and there was time to come up with fun ideas like this one.

1-1/2 cups chopped onion
   3 tablespoons vegetable oil
   4 cups diced peeled cooked potatoes
   8 bacon strips, cooked and crumbled
1/2 cup diced fully cooked ham
1/2 cup diced cooked roast beef
 12 eggs
   3 tablespoons minced fresh parsley
   2 teaspoons paprika
   1 teaspoon salt
1/2 teaspoon pepper
1/2 teaspoon garlic salt
1/2 teaspoon celery salt

In a 10-in. ovenproof skillet, cook onion in oil until tender. Add potatoes, bacon, ham and beef; heat through. Remove from the heat. In a bowl, beat eggs; stir in parsley and seasonings. Pour into skillet; stir gently to mix. Bake, uncovered, at 400° for 20-30 minutes or until a knife inserted near the center comes out clean. Cut into wedges to serve. **Yield:** 8-10 servings.

MEAL IN A MUFFIN PAN

Michelle Plumb, Montrose, Colorado
(PICTURED AT LEFT)

This meal-in-a-pan breakfast is ideal for busy weekday mornings. I just add fresh fruit and beverages.

   1 can (15 ounces) corned beef hash
   6 eggs
Salt and pepper to taste
   1 box (8-1/2 ounces) corn bread/muffin mix

Grease a 12-cup muffin pan. Divide hash into six of the cups; press into the bottom and up the sides to form a shell.

> **MEATY MEALS.** *Pictured at left, clockwise from the bottom: Farmhouse Omelet, Meal in a Muffin Pan and Bacon and Eggs Brunch (all recipes on this page).*

Break an egg into each shell; season with salt and pepper. Mix muffins according to package directions. Spoon batter into the other six cups. Bake at 400° for 15-20 minutes or until muffins are golden brown and eggs are cooked to desired doneness. **Yield:** 4-6 servings.

BACON AND EGGS BRUNCH

Lorna Herndon, Elyria, Ohio
(PICTURED AT LEFT)

This dish is perfect to serve guests because the eggs and Canadian bacon bake at the same time.

   2 tablespoons butter *or* margarine
 12 eggs
1/2 cup sour cream
1/2 cup milk
   1 teaspoon salt
   2 tablespoons sliced green onions
3/4 pound Canadian bacon, cut into 12 slices
1/4 cup maple syrup

Melt butter in an 11-in. x 7-in. x 2-in. baking dish in a 325° oven; tilt to coat bottom and sides. In a bowl, beat eggs, sour cream, milk and salt. Stir in onions. Pour into baking dish. Bake, uncovered, for 30 minutes or just until eggs are set. Place bacon in an 8-in. square baking dish. Pour syrup over. Cover and bake for 15 minutes or until heated through. Cut egg dish into squares and arrange on platter with Canadian bacon. **Yield:** 6 servings.

PORK SAUSAGE RING

Jeanee Volkmann, Waukesha, Wisconsin

Of all the recipes I've received, this one from my sister-in-law is my favorite. It's a fun way to serve scrambled eggs.

   2 eggs
1/2 cup milk
1-1/2 cups finely crushed saltines
   1 cup finely chopped apple
   2 pounds bulk pork sausage
Scrambled eggs

In a large bowl, beat eggs and milk. Add cracker crumbs, apple and sausage; mix well. Pat into a greased 6-cup ring mold. Bake at 350° for 1 hour and 15 minutes. Drain; unmold onto serving platter. Fill center with scrambled eggs. **Yield:** 10-12 servings.

SPICY BREAKFAST LASAGNA

Guthrie Torp Jr., Highlands Ranch, Colorado

It's fun to cook up something new for family and friends—especially when it gets rave reviews. When I brought this dish to our breakfast club at work, people said it really woke up their taste buds!

```
    3 cups (24 ounces) cottage cheese
  1/2 cup chopped fresh chives or 1/4 cup dried
        chives
  1/4 cup sliced green onions
    1 tablespoon butter or margarine
   18 eggs
  1/3 cup milk
  1/2 teaspoon salt
  1/4 teaspoon pepper
    8 lasagna noodles, cooked and drained
    4 cups frozen shredded hash browns
    1 pound bulk pork sausage, cooked and crumbled
    8 ounces sliced Monterey Jack cheese with
        jalapeno peppers
    8 ounces sliced Muenster cheese
```

In a bowl, combine cottage cheese, chives and onions; set aside. In a large skillet, melt butter. Beat eggs, milk, salt and pepper; pour into skillet. Cook and stir over medium heat until very loosely scrambled, about 5 minutes. Remove from heat; set aside. Line a greased 13-in. x 9-in. x 2-in. baking dish with four lasagna noodles. Top with 2 cups of hash browns, scrambled eggs, sausage and half of the cottage cheese mixture. Cover with Monterey Jack cheese. Repeat layers with the remaining lasagna noodles, hash browns and cottage cheese mixture. Top with Muenster cheese. Cover and chill 8 hours or overnight. Remove from the refrigerator 30 minutes before baking. Bake, uncovered, at 350° for 35-40 minutes or until a knife inserted near the center comes out clean. Let stand 5 minutes before cutting. **Yield:** 12-16 servings.

HAM 'N' CHEESE STRATA

Janet Wielhouwer, Grand Rapids, Michigan

This dish is so attractive and great-tasting that I love to make it for special brunches and showers. Because it's made the night before, I can relax in the morning before the guests arrive.

```
   15 slices white bread
    3 cups (12 ounces) shredded process American
        cheese
    2 tablespoons dried minced onion
    1 package (10 ounces) frozen chopped broccoli,
        cooked and drained
    2 cups diced fully cooked ham
    6 eggs, lightly beaten
3-1/2 cups milk
  1/4 teaspoon salt
  1/4 teaspoon dry mustard
Paprika
```

Using a doughnut cutter, cut 15 circles and holes from the bread; set aside. Tear leftover bread into small pieces and place in a greased 13-in. x 9-in. x 2-in. baking dish. Sprinkle cheese and onion over bread. Layer with broccoli and ham. Arrange bread circles and holes over ham. Combine eggs, milk, salt and mustard; pour over all. Cover and chill 8 hours or overnight. Remove from refrigerator 30 minutes before baking. Bake, uncovered, at 325° for 50 minutes; sprinkle with paprika. Bake an additional 10 minutes or until golden brown. Let stand 5 minutes before cutting. **Yield:** 12-16 servings.

BREAKFAST PIZZA

Kim Martin, Port Republic, Maryland

I love to cook and experiment with new recipes. When I first made this, my husband proclaimed it a definite "keeper"! This dish doesn't use traditional breakfast ingredients, but it's a surefire hit every time I serve it.

```
    1 tube (8 ounces) refrigerated crescent rolls
    1 pound bulk pork sausage
    1 can (4 ounces) sliced mushrooms, drained
    1 cup (4 ounces) shredded mozzarella cheese
    1 cup (4 ounces) shredded cheddar cheese
```

Separate crescent roll dough into eight triangles and place on an ungreased 12-in. round pizza pan with points toward the center. Press over bottom and up sides to form a crust; seal perforations. Bake at 350° for 10 minutes. Meanwhile, in a skillet, cook and crumble sausage. Drain; place over crust. Sprinkle with mushrooms and cheeses. Bake at 350° for 15 minutes or until cheese is melted. **Yield:** 8-10 servings.

PLEASING POTATO PIE

Elizabeth Leland, Los Alamos, New Mexico

After a hectic day of teaching junior high, I often headed to the quiet of my kitchen for peace! Now that I'm retired, cooking has replaced teaching as my first love. I especially like to serve this hearty dish for a relaxing weekend brunch.

```
    2 cups shredded peeled potatoes (about 1 pound)
1-1/2 cups (6 ounces) shredded cheddar cheese,
        divided
    1 teaspoon salt, divided
    4 eggs
  1/2 cup milk
    1 cup chopped fully cooked ham
  1/2 cup chopped onion
  1/2 teaspoon pepper
```

Combine potatoes, 1/2 cup cheese and 1/2 teaspoon salt. Press into the bottom and up the sides of a greased 9-in. pie plate. In a bowl, beat eggs and milk. Add ham, onion, pepper and remaining cheese and salt; pour over potato crust (dish will be very full). Bake at 350° for 45-50 minutes or until a knife inserted near the center comes out clean. Let stand 5 minutes before cutting. **Yield:** 4-6 servings.

EGGS ROYALE

Joan Downs, Lima, Ohio

My aunt gave this recipe to me after she served it at a wedding brunch. With muffins and fresh fruit, it's now my favorite breakfast entree. My hobbies are cooking and collecting cookbooks. In fact, I've collected so many books my dad built a bookshelf especially for them!

2-1/2 cups seasoned croutons
1-1/2 cups (6 ounces) shredded cheddar cheese
4 eggs
2 cups milk
1/2 teaspoon dry mustard
1/2 teaspoon salt
1/4 teaspoon onion powder
1/8 teaspoon pepper
10 bacon strips, cooked and crumbled

Place croutons in a greased 13-in. x 9-in. x 2-in. baking dish. Cover with cheese. In a bowl, beat eggs, milk, mustard, salt, onion powder and pepper; pour over cheese. Sprinkle with bacon. Cover and chill 8 hours or overnight. Remove from refrigerator 30 minutes before baking. Bake, uncovered, at 350° for 35-40 minutes or until a knife inserted near the center comes out clean. Let stand 5 minutes before cutting. **Yield:** 8-10 servings.

ASPARAGUS-CHICKEN PIE

Shirley Bartels, Peshtigo, Wisconsin

I stumbled upon this while I was rummaging through my large collection of recipes. It turned out to be a real find! I like to serve it for brunch and even as a light supper.

1 cup cooked fresh asparagus
1 unbaked pastry shell (9 inches)
1 cup chopped cooked chicken
3 bacon strips, cooked and crumbled
1/3 cup shredded process American cheese
3 eggs
1-1/3 cups light cream
2 teaspoons all-purpose flour
1/2 teaspoon salt
Paprika

Arrange asparagus in bottom of pie shell. Top with chicken, bacon and cheese. In a small bowl, beat eggs; stir in

cream, flour and salt. Pour into shell. Sprinkle with paprika. Bake at 375° for 45-50 minutes or until a knife inserted near the center comes out clean. Let stand 5 minutes before cutting. **Yield:** 6 servings.

RICE-CRUST QUICHE

Mary Ann Nelson, Redwood Falls, Minnesota

My favorite room in our house is the kitchen, where I love to carry on the country cooking traditions passed down to me through my grandmother and mother. I also enjoy sewing and crafting with my three daughters.

2-1/2 cups warm cooked rice
1/4 cup butter *or* margarine, melted
1-1/2 cups finely chopped fully cooked ham
1 cup (4 ounces) shredded cheddar cheese
1 cup (4 ounces) shredded Swiss cheese
Several drops hot pepper sauce
3 eggs
1/2 cup milk
1/8 teaspoon paprika
1/8 teaspoon garlic powder
1/8 teaspoon onion powder
Chopped fresh parsley

With the back of a spoon, press the rice into a greased 9-in. pie plate to form a crust. Drizzle with butter. Bake at 350° for 3 minutes; remove from the oven. Combine ham, cheeses and hot pepper sauce; sprinkle over rice. Beat eggs, milk, paprika, garlic powder and onion powder; pour over ham mixture. Sprinkle with parsley. Bake at 350° for 30 minutes or until a knife inserted near the center comes out clean. Let stand 5-10 minutes before cutting. **Yield:** 6 servings.

LAZY DAY CASSEROLE

Trish Parker, Blowing Rock, North Carolina

When I first served this wonderful brunch casserole at a family reunion a few years ago, I think I wrote out at least a dozen copies of the recipe! My husband and I enjoy country living in the beautiful Blue Ridge Mountains.

1/2 pound day-old Italian *or* French bread, sliced
1 pound bulk pork sausage, cooked and crumbled
8 eggs
2 cups milk
1/2 teaspoon pepper
8 ounces sliced Swiss cheese
1/4 cup chopped fresh parsley

Line the bottom of a greased 13-in. x 9-in. x 2-in. baking dish with bread. Sprinkle with sausage. Beat eggs, milk and pepper; pour over sausage. Press bread down with a spatula to absorb egg mixture. Top with cheese and parsley. Bake, uncovered, at 350° for 30-35 minutes or until a knife inserted near the center comes out clean. Let stand 5 minutes before cutting. **Yield:** 8 servings.

COUNTRY BRUNCH. *Clockwise from top right: Sausage Quiche, Savory Spinach Pie, Italian Sausage Casserole, Country Pepper Omelet Pie and Chili Relleno Mini Casseroles (all recipes on pages 10 and 11).*

COUNTRY PEPPER OMELET PIE

Sonja Blow, Groveland, California
(PICTURED ON PAGE 8)

I developed this recipe combining potatoes and eggs over 30 years ago as a way to satisfy my family's hearty appetites. The green and red peppers really add a festive flair to the table.

        1 cup chopped onion, *divided*
        3 tablespoons cooking oil
    3-1/2 cups frozen cubed hash brown potatoes
    1-1/2 teaspoons salt, *divided*
        1/2 teaspoon pepper, *divided*
        1/2 small sweet red pepper, chopped
        1/2 small green pepper, chopped
        2 tablespoons minced fresh parsley
        2 tablespoons butter *or* margarine
        1 cup (4 ounces) shredded Swiss cheese
        4 eggs
    1-1/4 cups milk
        1/4 teaspoon paprika

In a skillet, saute 1/2 cup onion in oil until tender. Add potatoes and half of the salt and pepper. Cook over medium heat until potatoes are thawed and softened, about 5 minutes. Pat potatoes into the bottom and up the sides of a greased 9-in. deep-dish pie plate. Bake at 400° for 20 minutes. Meanwhile, saute peppers, parsley and remaining onion in butter until tender. Spoon over potato crust. Top with cheese. In a bowl, beat eggs, milk, paprika and remaining salt and pepper. Pour over all. Bake, uncovered, at 400° for 30 minutes or until a knife inserted near the center comes out clean. Let stand 5 minutes before cutting. **Yield:** 6 servings.

CHILI RELLENO MINI CASSEROLES

Mary Jo Amos, Noel, Missouri
(PICTURED ON PAGE 8)

This recipe came about by accident 20 years ago. My sons had begged me to hurry up with breakfast so that we could play a game of catch. I whipped this up, spent time with my sons and then we all enjoyed our own spicy fun "casserole".

        4 flour tortillas (7 inches)
    1-1/2 tablespoons butter *or* margarine, melted
        2 cups (8 ounces) shredded Monterey Jack
            cheese
        1 tablespoon all-purpose flour
        1/4 teaspoon salt
        1/4 teaspoon pepper
        6 eggs, lightly beaten
        1 can (4 ounces) chopped green chilies
        1 garlic clove, minced
        1 tablespoon minced onion
    Salsa

Brush both sides of tortillas with butter. Place each tortilla in an individual ovenproof 10-oz. custard cup or casserole, pressing down in center to form a shell. In a bowl, combine cheese, flour, salt and pepper; set half aside. To the other half, add eggs, chilies, garlic and onion; pour into tortilla shells. Top with reserved cheese mixture. Bake, uncovered, at 325° for 25 minutes or until eggs are set. Let stand 5 minutes before serving. Serve with salsa. **Yield:** 4 servings.

ITALIAN SAUSAGE CASSEROLE

Nancy Robinson, Kansas City, Kansas
(PICTURED ON PAGE 9)

At the start of each week, my family is already looking forward to our traditional weekend breakfasts, when I serve warm and wonderful dishes such as this. The make-ahead convenience lets me relax with the family as the savory aroma fills the house.

        1 pound bulk pork sausage
        1 pound bulk Italian sausage
        1 medium green pepper, chopped
        1 cup sliced fresh mushrooms
        1/2 cup chopped onion
    2-1/2 cups onion and garlic croutons
        8 eggs
    1-1/2 cups milk
        1 cup (4 ounces) shredded mozzarella cheese
        1 cup (4 ounces) shredded cheddar cheese
        3 to 4 Roma tomatoes, thinly sliced
        1/2 cup shredded Parmesan cheese

In a large skillet, cook sausage, green pepper, mushrooms and onion until meat is browned and vegetables are tender; drain. Place croutons in a greased 13-in. x 9-in. x 2-in. baking dish; top with sausage mixture. Beat eggs and milk; pour over sausage. Cover and chill for 8 hours or overnight. Remove from refrigerator 30 minutes before baking. Bake, uncovered, at 300° for 1 hour. Sprinkle with the mozzarella and cheddar cheeses. Place tomato slices over top; sprinkle with Parmesan cheese. Bake 20 minutes longer or until a knife inserted near the center comes out clean. Let stand 5 minutes before cutting. **Yield:** 12 servings.

SAUSAGE QUICHE

Jennifer Polk, Lincoln, Nebraska
(PICTURED ON PAGE 9)

I often serve this hearty quiche to family and friends for special occasions. They just rave over the flavor.

        2 tubes (8 ounces *each*) refrigerated crescent rolls
        12 ounces mild link sausage, cooked and cut
            into 1/2-inch pieces
        1/2 cup chopped onion
        1 tablespoon butter *or* margarine

1 can (4 ounces) sliced mushrooms, drained
2 packages (3 ounces *each*) cream cheese, cut
    into 1/4-inch cubes
4 ounces process American cheese, cut into
    1/4-inch cubes
2 tablespoons chopped pimientos
6 eggs
2/3 cup light cream
1 tablespoon dried parsley flakes
1/2 teaspoon salt
1/2 teaspoon pepper
1/2 teaspoon garlic powder
Paprika

Unroll one tube of rolls; press dough onto the bottom and up the sides of a greased 11-in. x 7-in. x 2-in. baking pan to form a crust. Seal perforations. Sprinkle sausage over crust. In a skillet, saute onion in butter until tender; add mushrooms. Spoon over sausage. Top with cheeses and pimientos. In a bowl, beat eggs, cream, parsley, salt, pepper and garlic powder; pour over all. Unroll second tube of rolls; seal perforations. Cut dough into 1/2-in. lengthwise strips. Use strips to form a lattice crust over top of quiche. Sprinkle with paprika. Bake at 350° for 50-55 minutes; cover loosely with foil if browning too quickly. Let stand 10-15 minutes before cutting. **Yield:** 8-10 servings.

SAVORY SPINACH PIE

Pam Krenzke, Hilliard, Ohio
(PICTURED ON PAGE 9)

Even those who aren't morning people will break into smiles when they taste this super spinach pie. Served with cinnamon rolls and fresh fruit, it will surely get your day off to a sunny start!

1/4 cup chopped onion
2 tablespoons butter *or* margarine
1 package (10 ounces) frozen chopped spinach,
    thawed and well drained
1/4 to 1/2 teaspoon salt
1/4 teaspoon ground nutmeg
1 cup (8 ounces) cottage cheese
1/2 cup light cream
1/4 cup grated Parmesan cheese
3 eggs, lightly beaten
1 unbaked pastry shell (9 inches)

In a skillet, saute onion in butter. Remove from the heat; stir in spinach, salt and nutmeg. In a bowl, combine cottage cheese, cream, Parmesan cheese and eggs; mix well. Stir in spinach mixture. Pour into pie shell. Bake at 350° for 45-50 minutes or until a knife inserted near the center comes out clean. Let stand 5 minutes before cutting. **Yield:** 6 servings.

MAKE-AHEAD SCRAMBLED EGGS

Nancy Horn, Rogers City, Michigan

When my four sons, one daughter and their families come to visit, this egg dish is devoured in a hurry...even if I

double it! The Swiss cheese is a nice change from the usual cheddar cheese.

2 cups soft bread cubes (crusts removed)
1-3/4 cups milk
8 eggs, lightly beaten
3/4 teaspoon salt
1/8 teaspoon pepper
3 tablespoons butter *or* margarine, *divided*
2 cups (8 ounces) shredded Swiss cheese
1/4 cup dry bread crumbs
6 bacon strips, cooked and crumbled

Combine bread cubes and milk; let stand 5 minutes. Drain, reserving the excess milk. Place bread in a greased 8-in. square baking dish; set aside. Combine eggs and reserved milk; add salt and pepper. Melt 2 tablespoons butter in a large skillet; add egg mixture and cook just until eggs are set. Spoon over bread cubes. Top with Swiss cheese. Melt remaining butter; add bread crumbs. Sprinkle over cheese. Top with bacon. Cover and chill 8 hours or overnight. Remove from refrigerator 30 minutes before baking. Bake, uncovered, at 325° for 35 minutes or until heated through. Let stand 5 minutes before cutting. **Yield:** 8 servings.

PEPPER PURCHASE. *When selecting green and sweet red peppers, they should be firm and brightly colored. Refrigerate and use within 3 days.*

DOWN-ON-THE-FARM BREAKFAST

Cherie Sechrist, Red Lion, Pennsylvania

I've been making this dish for over 15 years, but it's still my husband's favorite and one that he requests most often. I'm not complaining, though. It's easy to prepare, and I love the combination of flavors as much as he does!

8 bacon strips, cut into 1/4-inch pieces
1 box (5-1/4 ounces) au gratin potatoes mix
2-1/4 cups boiling water
2/3 cup milk
1/4 cup chopped green pepper
2 tablespoons chopped onion
1/4 teaspoon dried thyme
6 eggs
Dash pepper
1/2 cup shredded cheddar cheese

Cook bacon in a large skillet until crisp. Drain, reserving 2 tablespoons drippings in the skillet with the bacon. Stir in contents of au gratin potato mix, water, milk, green pepper, onion and thyme. Bring to a boil, stirring frequently. Reduce heat; cover and simmer, stirring occasionally, for 20 minutes. Transfer to an ungreased 2-qt. baking dish. Make six indentations in potato mixture with a spoon. Break eggs into indentations. Sprinkle with pepper. Cover and bake at 350° for 20 minutes or until eggs reach desired doneness. Sprinkle with cheese. **Yield:** 6 servings.

ZUCCHINI BRUNCH PIE

Marjorie Boatman, Flat Rock, Illinois
(PICTURED AT LEFT)

After visiting our parents in the country one time, we came home laden with boxes of fresh vegetables. I shared them with a neighbor, who in turn shared this recipe with me. It has become one of our favorites—both to look at and to taste!

    4 cups sliced zucchini
    1 cup chopped onion
    1/4 cup butter *or* margarine
    2 eggs, lightly beaten
    2 cups (8 ounces) shredded mozzarella cheese
    1/2 cup chopped fresh parsley *or* 2 tablespoons
        dried parsley flakes
    1/2 teaspoon salt
    1/2 teaspoon pepper
    1/4 teaspoon garlic powder
    1/4 teaspoon dried basil
    1 can (8 ounces) refrigerated crescent rolls
    2 teaspoons prepared mustard

In a skillet, saute zucchini and onion in butter until tender, about 10 minutes. Remove from the heat; cool slightly. Stir in eggs, cheese, parsley, salt, pepper, garlic powder and basil. Separate the crescent rolls and press into an ungreased 10-in. pie plate to form a crust. Brush crust with mustard. Spoon zucchini mixture into crust. Bake at 375° for 10 minutes. Cover loosely with foil to prevent excess browning. Bake another 10 minutes or until a knife inserted near the center comes out clean. Let stand 5 minutes before cutting. **Yield:** 8 servings.

SAUSAGE SWIRLS

Gail Guild, Rome, New York
(PICTURED AT LEFT)

My husband is a chaplain, so our lives are a whirlwind of potluck brunches, lunches and dinners. These delicious sausage swirls really complement scrambled eggs and fruit salad.

    4 cups all-purpose flour
    1/4 cup cornmeal
    2 tablespoons sugar
    2 teaspoons baking powder
    1 teaspoon salt
    2/3 cup vegetable oil
    3/4 to 1 cup milk
    2 pounds uncooked bulk pork sausage

In a large bowl, combine the flour, cornmeal, sugar, baking powder and salt. Stir in oil until the mixture resembles coarse crumbs. Gradually stir in enough milk to form a

---

OVEN SPECIALTIES. *Pictured at left, clockwise from the top: Southern Eggs and Biscuits, Zucchini Brunch Pie and Sausage Swirls (all recipes on this page).*

---

soft dough. Turn onto a floured board; knead lightly for 30 seconds. Roll into two 16-in. x 10-in. rectangles. Crumble uncooked sausage over dough to within 1/2 in. on all sides. Carefully roll up from 16-in. end. Wrap in foil; chill for at least 1 hour. Cut into 1/2-in. slices; place 1 in. apart on ungreased baking sheets. Bake at 400° for 15-20 minutes or until lightly browned. Serve warm or cold. Store in the refrigerator. **Yield:** about 4 dozen.

SOUTHERN EGGS AND BISCUITS

Ruth Ward, Lexington, Tennessee
(PICTURED AT LEFT)

To me, nothing beats the flavor of Southern cooking, especially for breakfast! The rich flavor of these eggs served over homemade biscuits is a hearty way to start the day.

    10 hard-cooked eggs, sliced
    1 pound sliced bacon, diced
    1/3 cup all-purpose flour
    1/4 teaspoon salt
    1/8 teaspoon pepper
    4 cups milk
    2 cups cubed process American cheese
BISCUITS:
    1/2 cup shortening
    3 cups self-rising flour
1-1/4 cups buttermilk

Place eggs in the bottom of a greased 13-in. x 9-in. x 2-in. baking dish. In a large skillet, cook bacon until crisp. Drain, discarding all but 1/4 cup drippings. Sprinkle bacon over eggs. Stir flour, salt and pepper into reserved drippings; cook until bubbly. Gradually add milk; cook and stir until thickened and bubbly. Stir in cheese until melted; pour over eggs. For biscuits, cut shortening into flour until mixture resembles coarse crumbs. Stir in buttermilk; knead dough gently six to eight times. Roll out on a lightly floured surface to 1/2-in. thickness. Cut with a 2-1/2-in. biscuit cutter and place on a greased baking sheet. Bake biscuits and eggs at 400° for 25 minutes or until biscuits are golden brown. Serve eggs over biscuits. **Yield:** 6-8 servings.

CORNY BEEF BRUNCH

Kathleen Lutz, Steward, Illinois

My mother passed on her passion for cooking to me, my daughters and my grandchildren. One of my daughters shared this recipe with me after she made it for her first overnight guests after she was married.

    3 cans (14 ounces *each*) corned beef hash
    12 slices (1 ounce *each*) American cheese
    12 eggs
    1/2 teaspoon pepper

Spread hash in the bottom of a greased 13-in. x 9-in. x 2-in. baking dish. Layer cheese slices over hash. Beat eggs and pepper; pour over top. Bake at 350° for 35-40 minutes or until a knife inserted near the center comes out clean. **Yield:** 8-10 servings.

EASTER STUFFED EGGS
Kathy Christiansen, Whitefish, Montana

Most people dread all the leftover hard-cooked eggs they have at Easter. But not me! That's when I usually prepare one of my family's favorite dishes. The shrimp and curry powder give great flavor to ordinary eggs.

6 hard-cooked eggs
3 tablespoons mayonnaise
1 teaspoon grated onion
1 teaspoon salt, *divided*
1/8 teaspoon pepper
1 can (4-1/4 ounces) shrimp, drained, *divided*
4 tablespoons butter *or* margarine, melted, *divided*
3 tablespoons all-purpose flour
1-1/2 teaspoons curry powder
2 cups milk
1/4 cup crushed cornflakes

Cut eggs in half lengthwise. Set whites aside. In a bowl, mash yolks. Add mayonnaise, onion, 1/2 teaspoon salt and pepper. Chop 1/4 cup of shrimp; add to yolks. Mix well; spoon into egg white halves. Place in a greased 8-in. square baking dish; set aside. In a saucepan, blend 3 tablespoons of butter, flour, curry and remaining salt until smooth. Add milk; cook and stir over medium heat until smooth and thickened. Add remaining shrimp. Pour over eggs. Mix crumbs with remaining butter; sprinkle on top. Bake at 375° for 20 minutes or until heated through. **Yield:** 4-6 servings.

ALL-IN-ONE EGG CASSEROLE
Carol Trotter, Inman, South Carolina

I've had this unique recipe for years. It's always a hit at our house because it combines eggs, bacon, cheese, vegetables and bread all in one pan. I enjoy cooking for my husband of 31 years, two sons, one daughter and two grandsons.

10 bacon strips, diced
1 cup sliced fresh mushrooms
1/2 cup sliced green onions
1/4 cup butter *or* margarine
1/4 cup all-purpose flour
1/4 teaspoon salt
1/4 teaspoon pepper
2 cups milk
1-1/2 cups (6 ounces) shredded cheddar cheese
SCRAMBLED EGGS:
8 eggs
1/2 cup milk
1/2 teaspoon pepper
1/4 teaspoon salt
4 English muffins, split, toasted and lightly buttered
2 tablespoons minced fresh parsley

In a skillet, cook bacon until crisp. Remove bacon and set aside; discard all but 2 tablespoons of drippings. Saute mushrooms and onions in drippings until tender; set aside.

In a saucepan, melt butter. Stir in the flour, salt and pepper until smooth; cook until bubbly. Gradually stir in milk and cheese; cook and stir until thickened. Stir in bacon, mushrooms and onions; remove from the heat and set aside. For scrambled eggs, beat eggs, milk, pepper and salt; pour into a greased skillet. Cook and stir gently until eggs are set. Remove from the heat and set aside. Cut English muffin halves in half again. Place in the bottom and up the sides of a greased 11-in. x 7-in. x 2-in. baking dish. Cover with half of the cheese sauce. Spoon eggs over all; top with remaining sauce. Sprinkle with parsley. Bake, uncovered, at 325° for 20-25 minutes or until bubbly. Let stand 5 minutes before serving. **Yield:** 4-6 servings.

SPANISH-STYLE BREAKFAST BAKE
Dorothy Pritchett, Wills Point, Texas

Where I live in Texas, there are a lot of Mexican and Spanish influences in the local cooking. This interesting combination of rice, chili sauce, eggs and green peppers really adds some punch to your breakfast.

4 cups cooked long grain rice
2 cups (8 ounces) shredded cheddar cheese, *divided*
12 bacon strips, cooked and crumbled, *divided*
1 can (15 ounces) tomato sauce
1/2 cup bottled chili sauce
12 eggs
12 thinly sliced green pepper rings

In a bowl, combine rice, 1-1/2 cups cheese, 1/2 cup bacon, tomato sauce and chili sauce. Pat firmly into a greased 13-in. x 9-in. x 2-in. baking dish. Using the back of a spoon, make twelve 2-in. wells in the rice mixture. Cover and bake at 350° for 25 minutes. Remove from the oven; break an egg into each well. Press a green pepper ring around each egg. Cover and bake for another 30-35 minutes or until eggs reach desired doneness. Sprinkle with remaining cheese and bacon; cover and let stand 5-10 minutes or until cheese melts. **Yield:** 12 servings.

ZUCCHINI OVEN OMELET
Donnabelle Martin, Goshen, Indiana

Having been married for 50 years, I've had a lot of experience cooking meals for family and friends. They enjoy whatever I make, but this variation of a standard omelet is everyone's favorite.

2 cups chopped zucchini
1/4 cup chopped green pepper
1/4 cup cooking oil
6 eggs, lightly beaten
2 tablespoons grated Parmesan cheese
1 tablespoon light cream
1 tablespoon butter *or* margarine, melted
1/2 teaspoon salt
1/8 teaspoon pepper
1/2 cup shredded cheddar cheese

In a 10-in. ovenproof skillet, saute zucchini and green pepper in oil until tender, about 3 minutes. Combine eggs, Parmesan cheese, cream, butter, salt and pepper; pour over the vegetable mixture. Cook and stir gently for 3 minutes or until eggs are set on bottom. Top with cheese. Bake at 350° for 5-7 minutes or until eggs are set and cheese is melted. **Yield:** 4-6 servings.

GOLDEN COUNTRY GRITS

Sharon Stovall, Greenville, Kentucky

Although I was born and raised in the South, I never really cared for this truly Southern dish. But one day I was poring over my mother's collection of recipes, saw this and decided to give it a try. I've been a grits lover ever since!

> 4 cups cooked grits
> 1 cup (4 ounces) shredded sharp cheddar cheese
> 2 eggs, lightly beaten
> 1/4 cup butter *or* margarine, melted
> 1 tablespoon minced fresh parsley
> 1/2 teaspoon salt

In a large bowl, combine all of the ingredients. Pour into a greased 1-1/2-qt. baking dish. Bake, uncovered, at 350° for 30 minutes. **Yield:** 8-10 servings.

ITALIAN BREAKFAST CASSEROLES

Brenda Keeney, Spring Grove, Pennsylvania

My family just loves Italian food. So when I first whipped up this recipe using leftover spaghetti sauce, my family was delighted.

> 4 medium red potatoes, sliced
> 2 tablespoons cooking oil
> 8 eggs, lightly beaten
> 1 tablespoon butter *or* margarine
> 1/2 pound thinly sliced fully cooked ham, diced
> 2 cups prepared spaghetti sauce
> 1/2 cup *each* shredded cheddar and
>   mozzarella cheese

In a skillet, fry potatoes in oil until tender, about 10-15 minutes. Place in the bottom of four individual 16-oz. baking dishes. In the same skillet, scramble eggs in butter until set; spoon over potatoes. Top with ham. Pour 1/2 cup spaghetti sauce into each casserole; sprinkle with cheese. Bake at 350° for 20 minutes or until hot and bubbly. **Yield:** 4 servings.

CORNED BEEF HASH AND EGGS

Rick Skildum, Maple Grove, Minnesota

Sunday breakfasts have always been special in our house. It's fun to get in the kitchen and cook with the kids. No matter how many new recipes we try, the kids always rate this "No. 1"!

> 1 package (32 ounces) frozen cubed hash browns
> 1-1/2 cups chopped onion
> 1/2 cup vegetable oil

> 4 to 5 cups chopped cooked corned beef
> 1/2 teaspoon salt
> 8 eggs
> Salt and pepper to taste
> 2 tablespoons minced fresh parsley

In a large ovenproof skillet, cook hash browns and onion in oil until potatoes are browned and onion is tender. Remove from the heat; stir in corned beef and salt. Make eight wells in the hash browns. Break one egg into each well. Sprinkle with salt and pepper. Cover and bake at 325° for 20-25 minutes or until eggs reach desired doneness. Garnish with parsley. **Yield:** 8 servings.

SOUTHWESTERN EGG CASSEROLE

Sandra Greaves, Yuma, Arizona

The more time I spend in the kitchen, the happier I am! These baked eggs with a true Southwestern flavor are perfect to serve when entertaining overnight guests.

> 10 eggs
> 1/2 cup all-purpose flour
> 1 teaspoon baking powder
> 1/8 teaspoon salt
> 4 cups (16 ounces) shredded Monterey Jack cheese
> 2 cups (16 ounces) cottage cheese
> 1/2 cup butter *or* margarine, melted
> 2 cans (4 ounces *each*) chopped green chilies

In a large bowl, beat eggs. Combine flour, baking powder and salt; stir into eggs (batter will be lumpy). Add cheeses, butter and chilies. Pour into a greased 13-in. x 9-in. x 2-in. baking dish. Bake, uncovered, at 350° for 35-40 minutes or until a knife inserted near the center comes out clean. Let stand 5 minutes before cutting. **Yield:** 10-12 servings.

FLUFFY BAKED EGGS AND BACON

Cindy Bennett, Nova, Ohio

When I was student-teaching in Columbus, Ohio, some home economics students were always eager to share their creations with me...even their failures! This recipe was just one of their tasty successes, and it became a hit in my family.

> 1/2 pound sliced bacon, cut into 1-inch pieces
> 1/2 cup chopped onion
> 3 eggs
> 1-1/4 cups milk
> 1/2 cup buttermilk biscuit mix
> 1/4 teaspoon salt
> 1/8 teaspoon pepper
> 1/2 cup shredded cheddar cheese

In a skillet, cook bacon until almost crisp; add onion. Cook, stirring frequently, until bacon is crisp and onion is tender. Drain. Transfer to a 1-1/2-qt. casserole. In a mixing bowl, beat eggs, milk, biscuit mix, salt and pepper until almost smooth. Slowly pour over bacon and onion. Bake, uncovered, at 375° for 30 minutes or until a knife inserted near the center comes out clean. Sprinkle with cheese; let stand 5 minutes before cutting. **Yield:** 6 servings.

HEARTY EGG CASSEROLE

Mike Yaeger, Brookings, South Dakota
(PICTURED AT RIGHT)

Here in the middle of cattle country, our days always seem to be busy. This dish is true to its name—it's filling and keeps us going all morning. We also like to serve it to guests to give them a taste of true country cooking.

>   1 pound bulk pork sausage
>   1/2 cup chopped onion
>   1-1/2 cups (6 ounces) shredded cheddar cheese, *divided*
>   1 package (10 ounces) frozen chopped spinach, thawed and well drained
>   1 jar (4-1/2 ounces) sliced mushrooms, drained
>   12 eggs
>   2 cups heavy cream
>   1/4 teaspoon ground nutmeg

In a skillet, cook sausage and onion until the sausage is browned and the onion is tender; drain. Remove from the heat; stir in 1 cup cheese, spinach and mushrooms. Transfer to a greased 13-in. x 9-in. x 2-in. baking dish. In a bowl, beat eggs. Add cream and nutmeg; mix well. Pour over sausage mixture. Bake, uncovered, at 350° for 35-40 minutes or until a knife inserted near the center comes out clean. Sprinkle with remaining cheese. Let stand 5 minutes before cutting. **Yield:** 12 servings.

BRUNCH ENCHILADAS

Pat O'Brien, Soquel, California
(PICTURED AT RIGHT)

This recipe takes me back to when my grandmother would visit. While she prepared one of her delicious meals, she'd give me dough to make my own tortillas. With such "tasty" memories, it's no surprise this is my most asked-for recipe!

>   2 cups ground fully cooked ham
>   1/2 cup sliced green onions
>   1/2 cup finely chopped green pepper
>   2 tablespoons cooking oil
>   8 flour tortillas (7 inches)
>   2-1/2 cups (10 ounces) shredded cheddar cheese, *divided*
>   4 eggs
>   2 cups light cream
>   1 tablespoon all-purpose flour
>   1/4 teaspoon garlic powder
>   2 to 3 drops hot pepper sauce
> Salsa
> Sour cream

In a skillet, saute ham, onions and green pepper in oil until vegetables are tender. Place 1/3 cup down the center of each tortilla; top with 3 tablespoons cheese. Roll up and place seam side down in a greased 11-in. x 7-in. x 2-in. baking dish. In a bowl, beat the eggs. Add cream, flour, garlic powder and hot pepper sauce; mix well. Pour over tortillas. Cover and chill 8 hours or overnight. Re-

move from refrigerator 30 minutes before baking. Bake, uncovered, at 350° for 45-50 minutes or until a knife inserted near the center comes out clean. Sprinkle with remaining cheese. Let stand 5 minutes. Serve with salsa and sour cream. **Yield:** 4 servings.

WILD RICE QUICHE

Glenna Tooman, Boise, Idaho
(PICTURED AT RIGHT)

When you're short on time, this long-on-flavor quiche is just right! It's perfect for hectic morning meals because the sausage and rice can be cooked ahead of time.

>   1/2 pound bulk pork sausage, cooked and crumbled
>   1 cup wild rice, cooked and cooled
>   1 cup (4 ounces) shredded cheddar cheese
>   1-3/4 cups milk
>   1 cup buttermilk biscuit mix
>   4 eggs

In a greased 10-in. pie plate, layer sausage, rice and cheese. In a bowl, combine milk, baking mix and eggs; beat until smooth. Pour evenly over cheese. Bake at 400° for 30-35 minutes or until a knife inserted near the center comes out clean. Let stand 5 minutes before cutting. **Yield:** 6-8 servings.

BREAKFAST BREAD PUDDING

Nadeen Kovanda, Columbus, Montana

I first made this breakfast version of bread pudding for our annual Memorial Day breakfast more than 10 years ago. I'm eager to try new recipes each year, but my friends and family love this so much they won't let me make anything else!

>   1/4 cup butter *or* margarine, melted
>   3 eggs, *separated*
>   2 cups milk
>   1/2 teaspoon dry mustard
>   1/2 teaspoon salt
>   1/4 teaspoon cayenne pepper
>   9 slices bread, cut into 1/2-inch cubes
>   3 cups (12 ounces) shredded cheddar cheese

In a large bowl, combine butter, egg yolks, milk, mustard, salt and cayenne pepper. Stir in bread cubes and cheese. In another bowl, beat egg whites until soft peaks form; fold into bread mixture. Pour into a greased 9-in. square baking dish. Cover and chill for 8 hours or overnight. Remove from refrigerator 30 minutes before baking. Bake, uncovered, at 350° for 40-45 minutes or until a knife inserted near the center comes out clean. Let stand 5 minutes before cutting. **Yield:** 6-8 servings.

HEARTY HELPINGS. *Pictured at right, top to bottom: Hearty Egg Casserole, Brunch Enchiladas and Wild Rice Quiche (all recipes on this page).*

HOME-STYLE HOMINY CASSEROLE

Helen Ratliff, Louisville, Kentucky

When my six children were growing up, I was always looking for recipes that were filling as well as tasty. So when I came upon this dish years ago, I knew I had to try it. My family loves this casserole so much I've also been known to make it for supper.

   1 pound bulk pork sausage
   1 can (15-1/2 ounces) white hominy, drained
  12 eggs
1/4 cup milk
1/4 teaspoon pepper
   8 ounces process American cheese, sliced

In a large skillet, brown and crumble sausage; drain. Add hominy; stir until heated through, about 5 minutes. In a large bowl, beat eggs, milk and pepper. Add to hominy mixture; cook and stir gently until eggs are set. Pour into a greased 2-qt. baking dish. Cover with cheese slices. Place under broiler until cheese is melted. **Yield:** 8-10 servings.

INDIVIDUAL EGG BAKES

Bettie Tuttle, Grants Pass, Oregon

Don't sell this simple but delicious recipe short. It's been a hit with my friends and family for years. I plan to make a few extra each time because no one can seem to eat enough of them!

   8 bacon strips
   1 cup ketchup, chili-pepper ketchup *or* salsa
   8 eggs
Salt and pepper to taste
Chopped fresh parsley, optional

Partially cook bacon in microwave or oven until about halfway done (do not overcook); drain. Spray eight 10-oz. custard cups with nonstick cooking spray. Line each cup with one bacon strip. Spoon 2 tablespoons ketchup or salsa on top of bacon. Break one egg into each cup; season with salt and pepper. Place cups on a baking sheet. Bake, uncovered, at 375° for 18-20 minutes or until eggs reach desired doneness. Let stand 2 minutes. Run a knife around edge of cups; slip eggs out of cups onto a serving platter. Spoon sauce from the custard cups over the eggs. Garnish with parsley if desired. **Yield:** 8 servings.

CHEESY EGG CASSEROLE

Dawn Reeve, Salt Lake City, Utah

This dish is perfect for potlucks because it looks so pretty on the table and, best of all, it can be made ahead of time. Although I don't live in the country, my family and I love the country flavor of this hearty egg casserole.

   1 pound Monterey Jack cheese, shredded
   1 tablespoon all-purpose flour

   2 cups (8 ounces) shredded sharp cheddar cheese
   1 pound sliced bacon, cooked and crumbled
  12 eggs
   1 cup milk

Toss Monterey Jack cheese with flour; place in the bottom of a greased 13-in. x 9-in. x 2-in. baking dish. Top with cheddar cheese; sprinkle with bacon. Beat eggs and milk; pour over all. Cover and chill 8 hours or overnight. Remove from refrigerator 30 minutes before baking. Bake, uncovered, at 325° for 40-45 minutes or until a knife inserted near the center comes out clean. Let stand 5 minutes before cutting. **Yield:** 12-16 servings.

CHRISTMAS MORNING PIE

Sally Harlan, Charleston, South Carolina

I first made this festive breakfast pie when entertaining friends on Christmas morning. Each year I was asked to make my famous "Christmas Morning Pie" and the name stuck! But because of its great flavor, I make it year-round.

   1 pound bulk pork sausage with sage, cooked and crumbled
   1 cup (4 ounces) shredded Swiss cheese
   1 cup (4 ounces) shredded cheddar cheese
   2 unbaked pastry shells (9 inches)
   6 eggs, lightly beaten
   1 cup milk
1/2 cup chopped onion
1/3 cup chopped sweet red pepper
1/3 cup chopped green pepper

In a bowl, combine sausage and cheeses. Place half of mixture in each pastry shell. Combine eggs, milk, onion and peppers. Pour half over sausage in each shell. Bake at 350° for 55-60 minutes or until a knife inserted near the center comes out clean. Let stand 5 minutes before cutting. **Yield:** 12-16 servings.

OVERNIGHT SAUSAGE AND GRITS

Susan Ham, Cleveland, Tennessee

This recipe is so appealing because it can be prepared the night before and then popped into the oven an hour before you want to eat. This hearty dish works well as a side dish with pancakes or waffles or can be served as the main course.

   3 cups hot cooked grits
   1 pound bulk pork sausage, cooked and crumbled
2-1/2 cups (10 ounces) shredded cheddar cheese
   3 eggs
1-1/2 cups milk
   3 tablespoons butter *or* margarine, melted
1/4 teaspoon garlic powder

In a large bowl, mix grits, sausage and cheese. Beat the eggs and milk; stir into grits. Add butter and garlic powder. Transfer to a greased 13-in. x 9-in. x 2-in. baking dish. Cover and chill 8 hours or overnight. Remove from the refrigerator 30 minutes before baking. Bake, uncovered, at 350° for 1 hour or until a knife inserted near the center comes out clean. Let stand 5 minutes before cutting. **Yield:** 10-12 servings.

QUICK QUICHE CUPS

Susan Voigt, Plymouth, Minnesota

When I host a brunch or shower, this is the recipe I reach for most often. Not only are the individual quiche cups easy to make, they look so impressive on the table.

    1 package (3 ounces) cream cheese, softened
    2/3 cup sour cream
    2 eggs, lightly beaten
    1/2 cup shredded Swiss cheese
    4 bacon strips, cooked and crumbled
    2 tablespoons finely chopped sweet red pepper
    1/4 teaspoon dried oregano
    1 tube (10 ounces) refrigerated biscuits

In a mixing bowl, beat cream cheese and sour cream until smooth. Add eggs; mix well. Stir in Swiss cheese, bacon, red pepper and oregano; set aside. Separate dough into 10 biscuits; flatten into 5-in. circles. Press each into the bottom and up the sides of a greased muffin cup. Divide the egg mixture among biscuit-lined muffin cups, using about 2 tablespoons for each. Bake at 375° for 18-20 minutes or until a knife inserted near the center comes out clean. Let stand 5 minutes before removing from tin and serving. **Yield:** 10 servings.

HAM AND POTATO CASSEROLE

Alice Clark, Quincy, Florida

I teach Sunday school to adult women. Once a year I invite them to my home for a special brunch. Of all the food I've served to them over the past 6 years, this recipe stands out as the favorite.

    1 package (26 ounces) frozen shredded hash
      browns
    3 tablespoons cooking oil
    2 cups diced fully cooked ham
    2 cans (10-3/4 ounces each) condensed cream of
      potato soup, undiluted
    2 cups (16 ounces) sour cream
    2 cups (8 ounces) shredded sharp cheddar
      cheese, divided
    1/2 cup (4 ounces) shredded Parmesan cheese

In a large skillet, fry hash browns in oil until browned. Remove from heat, stir in ham, soup, sour cream, 1-1/2 cups cheddar cheese and Parmesan cheese. Pour into a greased 13-in. x 9-in. x 2-in. baking dish. Sprinkle with remaining cheddar cheese. Bake, uncovered, at 350° for 35-40 minutes. **Yield:** 8-10 servings.

EYE-OPENER RANCH EGGS

Audrey Thibodeau, Fountain Hills, Arizona

Here in the Southwest, we like our food spicy, so these sunny-side up eggs provide the right amount of zip! And hot buttered flour tortillas are a nice alternative to regular bread.

    2 large tomatoes, chopped
    1 can (2.8 ounces) french-fried onions, *divided*
    1 can (4 ounces) chopped green chilies
    1/2 to 1 jalapeno pepper, minced
    6 eggs
Salt and pepper to taste
    1 cup (4 ounces) shredded Monterey Jack cheese
    1/4 cup sliced ripe olives
Flour tortillas, warmed and buttered, optional

In a large bowl, combine the tomatoes, half of the onions, chilies and jalapeno pepper. Place in a greased 8-in. square baking dish. Break eggs carefully on top. Sprinkle with salt and pepper. Cover with cheese and olives. Bake, uncovered, at 400° for 15-20 minutes or until the eggs are set. Sprinkle with remaining onions. Serve with hot buttered tortillas if desired. **Yield:** 4-6 servings.

SLUMBER PARTY PIE

Jane Seitz, Catawba, North Carolina

This breakfast pizza with a unique name is great to serve to teenagers after an all-night slumber party. It's one of my favorite dishes because it uses ingredients I often keep on hand.

    1/2 pound bulk pork sausage
    1 tube (8 ounces) refrigerated crescent rolls
    1 cup frozen shredded hash brown potatoes
    1 cup (4 ounces) shredded cheddar cheese
    5 eggs
    1/4 cup milk
    1/2 teaspoon salt
    1/8 teaspoon pepper
    2 tablespoons grated Parmesan cheese

In a skillet, cook and crumble the sausage until browned; drain. Separate crescent roll dough into eight triangles and place on an ungreased 12-in. round pizza pan with points toward center. Press over bottom and up sides to form a crust; seal perforations. Spoon sausage over crust. Top with potatoes and cheddar cheese. In a bowl, beat eggs, milk, salt and pepper; pour evenly over all. Sprinkle with Parmesan cheese. Bake at 375° for 20-25 minutes. **Yield:** 6-8 servings.

ASPARAGUS QUICHE

Sharon Skildum, Maple Grove, Minnesota
(PICTURED AT RIGHT)

My husband and I are avid sailors. So before we head out to the lake on chilly mornings, I like to prepare this hearty quiche, along with coffee and fresh-from-the-oven muffins for a warm wake-up.

     1 pound fresh asparagus
     1 teaspoon salt
     1 unbaked pastry shell (10 inches)
     1 egg white, lightly beaten
     2 cups (8 ounces) shredded Swiss cheese
    10 bacon strips, cooked and crumbled
     4 eggs
  1-1/2 cups light cream
   1/4 teaspoon ground nutmeg
   1/4 teaspoon salt
Pinch pepper
Cherry tomatoes, halved

Cut eight asparagus spears 4 in. long for garnish. Cut remaining asparagus into 1/2-in. pieces, using only tender parts of stalks. Boil 1 qt. of water in a large saucepan; add salt and all of the asparagus. Return to a boil. Reduce heat; cover and simmer for 5 minutes. Drain and rinse asparagus. Brush bottom of pastry shell with egg white. In a bowl, combine cut asparagus, Swiss cheese and bacon; mix gently. Place in bottom of pastry shell. In another bowl, beat eggs, cream, nutmeg, salt and pepper until smooth. Pour into shell. Bake, uncovered, at 400° for 35-40 minutes or until a knife inserted near the center comes out clean. Arrange the asparagus spears, spoke fashion, on top of quiche; place cherry tomato halves between spokes. **Yield:** 6-8 servings.

TENDER AND TASTY. *The tenderness of asparagus is determined by color, not by the thinness of the spears. The more green (or white) the asparagus is, the more tender it will be.*

STUFFED BREAKFAST LOAF

Frances Contestable, Crockett, California
(PICTURED AT RIGHT)

My favorite hobby for the past 38 years has been collecting cookbooks. Presently I have close to 500! I found this recipe in one of my favorite books and it's been part of our holiday breakfast tradition for years.

     1 unsliced round French *or* sourdough bread
       (1 pound)
     4 ounces bulk Italian sausage
     4 ounces bulk pork sausage
   1/4 cup chopped onion
   1/4 cup chopped green pepper

   1/4 cup sliced fresh mushrooms
     4 eggs, lightly beaten
   1/2 cup *each* shredded Monterey Jack and
       cheddar cheese

Cut bread in half horizontally; hollow out top and bottom, leaving a 3/4-in. shell. Save removed bread for another use. In a large skillet, cook sausage, onion, green pepper and mushrooms until sausage is no longer pink and vegetables are tender. Remove mixture and set aside; drain all but 1 tablespoon of drippings. Add eggs; cook and stir gently until set. Stir in sausage mixture; remove from the heat. Place bread bottom on a large sheet of foil. Combine cheeses; sprinkle half in the bread bottom. Spoon in egg mixture and cover with remaining cheese. Replace bread top and wrap tightly with foil. Bake at 400° for 25 minutes or until filling is heated through. **Yield:** 4-6 servings.

EGGSQUISITE BREAKFAST CASSEROLE

Bee Fischer, Jefferson, Wisconsin
(PICTURED AT RIGHT)

I developed this recipe over 20 years ago. The rich warm sauce tastes especially great on cold winter mornings. I hope your family enjoys it as much as mine!

     1 pound sliced bacon, diced
     2 packages (4-1/2 ounces *each*) sliced dried beef,
       cut into thin strips
     1 can (4 ounces) sliced mushrooms, drained
   1/2 cup all-purpose flour
   1/8 teaspoon pepper
     4 cups milk
    16 eggs
     1 cup evaporated milk
   1/4 teaspoon salt
   1/4 cup butter *or* margarine
Chopped fresh parsley, optional

In a large skillet, cook bacon until crisp. Remove bacon to paper towel to drain; discard all but 1/4 cup drippings. Add beef, mushrooms, flour and pepper to the drippings; cook until thoroughly combined. Gradually add milk; cook and stir until thickened. Stir in bacon; set aside. In a large bowl, beat eggs, evaporated milk and salt. In another skillet, melt butter. Add eggs; cook and stir gently until eggs are set. Place half of the eggs in a greased 13-in. x 9-in. x 2-in. baking dish; pour half the sauce over the eggs. Spoon on remaining eggs, then remaining sauce. Cover and bake at 300° for 45-50 minutes or until heated through. Let stand 5 minutes before serving. Garnish with parsley if desired. **Yield:** 12-16 servings.

SPRINGTIME STARTERS. *Pictured at right, clockwise from the top: Eggsquisite Breakfast Casserole, Stuffed Breakfast Loaf and Asparagus Quiche (all recipes on this page).*

GOLDEN OVEN OMELET

Mrs. John Zones, Waterville, Washington

When I have many mouths to feed and little time on my hands, this is the recipe I reach for. Actually, I've made it so many times, I know it by heart!

- 1/4 cup butter *or* margarine, melted
- 18 eggs
- 1 cup milk
- 1 cup (8 ounces) sour cream
- 1/4 cup sliced green onions
- 2 teaspoons salt

Pour butter into a 13-in. x 9-in. x 2-in. baking dish. In a mixing bowl, beat eggs, milk, sour cream, onions and salt until smooth. Pour into pan. Bake, uncovered, at 325° for 30-35 minutes or until a knife inserted near the center comes out clean. Let stand 5 minutes. **Yield:** 12-14 servings.

SPICY SAUSAGE CASSEROLE

Margie Upchurch, Woodstock, Georgia

My family loves to sleep in on weekends, so they convinced me to serve brunch instead of breakfast. But it seems whenever the aroma of this dish fills the house, they wake up a little earlier!

- 2 cups cooked rice
- 1 pound bulk pork sausage, cooked and drained
- 1 can (6 ounces) sliced water chestnuts, drained
- 4 cups (16 ounces) shredded sharp cheddar cheese
- 1-1/2 cups chopped cooked broccoli

In a 2-qt. casserole, layer rice, sausage, water chestnuts, 1 cup cheese, broccoli and then remaining cheese. Bake, uncovered, at 375° for 30 minutes or until cheese is bubbly. **Yield:** 6-8 servings.

SAN JOSE TORTILLA PIE

Anne Boesiger, Billings, Montana

Because my husband is in the Navy, we've lived in many parts of the country and have had the great opportunity of trying different foods in each region. This is a family favorite served with fried potatoes and fruit.

- 6 corn tortillas (6 inches)
- Cooking oil
- Salt
- 1 pound ground beef
- 1 large onion, chopped
- 1 medium green pepper, chopped
- 1 garlic clove, minced
- 1 tablespoon chili powder
- 1 teaspoon dried oregano
- 1 teaspoon ground cumin
- 2 cups (8 ounces) shredded cheddar cheese
- 1 to 2 cans (4 ounces *each*) chopped green chilies

- 6 eggs
- 1-1/2 cups milk
- 1/2 teaspoon salt
- Sliced ripe olives, optional

Cut each tortilla into eight wedges. Saute a few at a time in hot oil until crisp. Drain on paper towels; sprinkle with salt. In a large skillet, cook ground beef, onion, green pepper and garlic until beef is browned and vegetables are tender; drain. Stir in chili powder, oregano and cumin. In a greased 13-in. x 9-in. x 2-in. baking dish, layer half of the tortilla wedges, half the meat mixture and half of the cheese. Sprinkle chilies evenly over cheese. Top with remaining meat and cheese. Tuck remaining tortilla wedges, point side up, around edge of dish. In a small bowl, beat eggs, milk and salt. Pour evenly over top. Bake, uncovered, at 375° for 25-30 minutes. Garnish with olives if desired. **Yield:** 10-12 servings.

WAKE-UP SANDWICHES

Kayla Thielen, Carroll, Iowa

Like most people, we always have leftover hard-cooked eggs after Easter. But my family doesn't mind because they know I'll be making these breakfast sandwiches.

- 4 ounces cream cheese, softened
- 2 tablespoons milk
- 1 package (2-1/2 ounces) sliced corned beef, chopped
- 1/2 cup shredded Swiss cheese
- 2 hard-cooked eggs, chopped
- 3 English muffins, split and toasted
- Sliced hard-cooked egg, optional
- Minced fresh parsley, optional

In a bowl, combine cream cheese and milk until smooth. Fold in corned beef, cheese and chopped eggs. Spread 1/3 cup mixture on each muffin half. Bake at 450° for 10-12 minutes or until heated through. If desired, garnish each half with an egg slice and parsley. **Yield:** 2-3 servings.

BRUNCH TIDBITS

Linda Lamberth, Tyler, Texas

I really enjoy cooking but rarely have the time during the week. So we treasure our weekend breakfasts, when I prepare special recipes like these tasty tidbits.

- 1-1/2 cups (6 ounces) shredded cheddar cheese
- 3/4 cup chopped green olives
- 3/4 cup chopped ripe olives
- 1/2 cup salad dressing *or* mayonnaise
- 1/4 cup sliced green onions
- 1/4 teaspoon pepper
- 4 English muffins, split

In a bowl, combine cheese, olives, salad dressing, onions and pepper. Spread on English muffins; cut into fourths. Place on an ungreased baking sheet and bake at 350° for 8-10 minutes or until bubbly. Or freeze and bake frozen at 350° for 18-20 minutes. **Yield:** 8 servings.

GROUND BEEF QUICHE

Vickie Tinsley, Boonville, Missouri

This hearty quiche is perfect to serve overnight guests because it's so easy to make. Your guests will love the delicious combination of beef and Swiss cheese.

    1/2 pound ground beef
    1/2 cup chopped onion
    1/2 teaspoon salt
    1/2 teaspoon dried oregano
    1/2 teaspoon garlic powder
    1/4 teaspoon pepper
      3 eggs
    1/2 cup milk
    1/2 cup mayonnaise
      1 cup (4 ounces) shredded cheddar cheese
      1 cup (4 ounces) shredded Swiss cheese
      1 unbaked pastry shell (9 inches)

In a skillet, cook ground beef and onion until beef is browned and onion is tender; drain. Stir in salt, oregano, garlic powder and pepper. In a bowl, beat eggs, milk and mayonnaise; stir into meat mixture. Fold in cheeses. Pour into pastry shell. Bake, uncovered, at 350° for 35 minutes or until a knife inserted near the center comes out clean. Let stand 5 minutes before cutting. **Yield:** 6 servings.

SPECIAL REQUEST CASSEROLE

Patsye Yonce, Ovid, New York

This has been a family favorite for years, and I made it often when my two children were growing up. The kids are now grown and away from home, but whenever they visit, they always put in a special request for this delicious cheesy dish.

     30 saltine crackers
      6 eggs, lightly beaten
      6 bacon strips, cooked and crumbled
      2 cups milk
      2 cups (8 ounces) shredded cheddar cheese
    1/4 cup butter *or* margarine, melted

Crumble crackers into a 11-in. x 7-in. x 2-in. baking dish. Combine remaining ingredients; pour over crackers. Cover and chill for 8 hours or overnight. Remove from refrigerator 30 minutes before baking. Bake, uncovered, at 325° for 45 minutes or until a knife inserted near the center comes out clean. Let stand 5 minutes before cutting. **Yield:** 8 servings.

CORNFLAKE BACON COOKIES

Lois McAtee, Oceanside, California

The older my four children got, the less time they seemed to make for breakfast. So I often kept these hearty cookies on hand for them to eat on the go.

    1/2 cup butter *or* margarine, softened
    3/4 cup sugar

      1 egg
      1 cup all-purpose flour
    1/4 teaspoon baking soda
     10 bacon strips, cooked and crumbled
      2 cups cornflakes
    1/2 cup raisins

In a mixing bowl, cream butter and sugar until light. Beat in egg. Combine flour and baking soda; gradually add to creamed mixture. Blend thoroughly. Stir in bacon, cornflakes and raisins. Drop by rounded tablespoonfuls 2 in. apart on ungreased baking sheets. Bake at 350° for 15-18 minutes or until golden brown. Store in the refrigerator. **Yield:** 2 dozen.

SAUSAGE STRATA

Lovetta Bothwell, Pisgah, Iowa

At our cafe, breakfast is probably our busiest time of day. So I need recipes that are easy to prepare. The seasoned croutons are a fast way to add great flavor.

    1-1/2 pounds bulk pork sausage, cooked and
            crumbled
        3 cups onion and garlic croutons
       18 eggs
        3 cups (12 ounces) shredded sharp cheddar
            cheese
        2 cups milk
    1-1/2 teaspoons salt
    Tomato slices, optional

Place sausage and croutons in a greased 13-in. x 9-in. x 2-in. baking dish. In a large bowl, beat eggs. Stir in cheese, milk and salt; pour into pan. Bake, uncovered, at 325° for 45-50 minutes or until a knife inserted near the center comes out clean. Let stand 5 minutes before cutting. Garnish with tomato slices if desired. **Yield:** 10-12 servings.

HAM AND CHEESE BISCUITS

Mrs. John Clark, Quincy, Florida

These specially stuffed biscuits are a must throughout the year. I get asked to make them for school parties, bridal luncheons and holiday get-togethers.

        2 packages heat and serve pull-apart rolls
            (24 rolls)
    1-1/2 pounds shaved fully cooked ham
        6 slices (6 to 8 ounces) Swiss cheese, quartered
      1/4 cup butter *or* margarine, melted
        1 tablespoon prepared mustard
      1/2 teaspoon Worcestershire sauce
        1 tablespoon poppy seeds

Separate rolls. Evenly divide ham and cheese into 24 portions and place in the center of each roll. Place in a greased 13-in. x 9-in. x 2-in. baking pan. Combine butter, mustard and Worcestershire sauce; mix well. Pour over rolls. Sprinkle with poppy seeds. Bake at 350° for 10-15 minutes. **Yield:** 6-8 servings.

Cookin' Up...
SKILLET SPECIALTIES

Put some sizzle into your breakfast with savory sausage and potato dishes. And for mighty "eggs-cellent" eating, try these deliciously different omelets and eggs.

VEGETABLE SCRAMBLED EGGS

Marilyn Ipson, Rogers, Arkansas
(PICTURED AT LEFT)

I like to have friends and family over for a special Sunday brunch, especially when there's a "big game" on television. These colorful eggs go perfectly with sausage, toasted English muffins and fresh fruit.

    4 eggs
    1/2 cup chopped green pepper
    1/4 cup milk
    1/4 cup sliced green onions
    1/2 teaspoon salt
    1/8 teaspoon pepper
    1 small tomato, chopped and seeded

In a small bowl, beat eggs. Add green pepper, milk, onions, salt and pepper. Pour into a lightly greased skillet. Cook and stir over medium heat until eggs are nearly set. Add the tomato; cook and stir until heated through. **Yield:** 2 servings.

HEARTY HAM OMELET

Debbie Troyer, Millersburg, Ohio
(PICTURED AT LEFT)

I came up with this delicious and filling omelet for my husband and daughters, who think breakfast is the best meal of the day. I love to cook and had the best teacher around...my mom!

    1 medium green pepper, chopped
    1/2 cup chopped fully cooked ham
    1 small onion, chopped
    1 can (4 ounces) sliced mushrooms, drained
    1 tablespoon butter *or* margarine
    6 eggs
    1/4 cup milk
    1 tablespoon minced fresh parsley
    1/4 teaspoon salt
    1/4 teaspoon pepper
    1 cup (4 ounces) shredded cheddar *or* process
    American cheese

> **SUPER SKILLETS.** *Pictured at left, clockwise from the top: Hearty Ham Omelet, Quick Sausage Gravy and Vegetable Scrambled Eggs (all recipes on this page).*

In a 12-in. nonstick skillet, cook green pepper, ham, onion and mushrooms in butter until tender; remove from skillet and set aside. In a mixing bowl, beat eggs with milk, parsley, salt and pepper. Pour into the skillet; cook over medium heat. As eggs set, lift edges, letting uncooked portion flow underneath. When eggs are set, spoon vegetable mixture over half the omelet. Top with half of the cheese. Fold omelet in half over filling. Sprinkle with remaining cheese. Cover 1-2 minutes or until cheese melts. Serve on a warm platter. **Yield:** 4 servings.

QUICK SAUSAGE GRAVY

Joan Daumeyer, Blanchester, Ohio
(PICTURED AT LEFT)

I thought everyone knew how to make sausage gravy until my husband, George, and I served it for a breakfast we hosted. It disappeared quickly, and everyone who tried it asked me for the recipe.

    1 pound bulk pork sausage
    2 tablespoons all-purpose flour
    1-3/4 cups milk
    6 warm biscuits, halved

In a skillet, brown and crumble sausage until fully cooked; drain. Sprinkle with flour and blend. Gradually add milk, stirring constantly. Bring to a boil; boil for 1 minute. Cook until thickened. Serve over biscuits. **Yield:** 6 servings.

CURRIED SCRAMBLED EGG

Lorraine Wiech, San Luis Obispo, California

When my doctor told me to eliminate salt from my diet, I thought I would never eat another egg again! But the chives and curry powder in this recipe pack the right amount of punch and add even more flavor to eggs than salt ever did.

    1 egg
    1 teaspoon water
    1 teaspoon finely chopped chives
    1/8 to 1/4 teaspoon curry powder
    1 teaspoon olive oil

In a small bowl, beat the egg, water, chives and curry powder. Pour oil into a small skillet; add egg mixture. Cook and stir gently over medium heat until egg is set. **Yield:** 1 serving.

SALMON SCRAMBLE

Janine Baker, Kansas City, Missouri

One morning years ago, my husband, Todd, and I whipped up this dish as a way to use leftover smoked salmon...it caught on! Now we always make extra portions of this tasty fish at dinner so we can have our family favorite in the morning.

   8 eggs
3/4 cup milk
1/2 teaspoon salt
1/8 teaspoon pepper
   1 can (7-1/2 ounces) pink salmon, drained *or* 1 cup smoked salmon, flaked and cartilage removed
1/2 cup shredded Monterey Jack cheese
1/4 cup minced fresh parsley

In a bowl, beat eggs, milk, salt and pepper. Stir in salmon, cheese and parsley. In a greased skillet, cook and stir gently over medium heat until eggs are set, about 3-5 minutes. **Yield:** 4-6 servings.

WAKE-UP BACON OMELET

Mary Rayunec, Homosassa, Florida

The hot pepper sauce adds the right amount of zip to this delicious omelet. And because it's so easy to prepare, it's perfect for both hurried weekday breakfasts and leisurely weekend brunches.

   2 to 4 bacon strips, diced
2 eggs
2 tablespoons water
2 teaspoons fresh *or* dried chives
3 to 5 drops hot pepper sauce
Salt and pepper to taste

In an 8-in. nonstick skillet, cook bacon until crisp. Remove bacon to paper towel to drain; discard drippings. In a small bowl, beat eggs; add water, chives, hot pepper sauce, salt, pepper and bacon. Pour into the same skillet; cook over medium heat. As eggs set, lift edges, letting uncooked portion flow underneath. When eggs are set, fold omelet in thirds. **Yield:** 1 serving.

FARMER'S COUNTRY BREAKFAST

June Smith, Byron Center, Michigan

When my family has a busy day ahead of them, I prepare a hearty breakfast to get them through the morning. Packed with pork sausage and potatoes, this one-skillet dish surely fits the bill.

   6 ounces bulk pork sausage
1-1/2 cups frozen hash brown potatoes
1/4 cup chopped onion
   6 eggs
1/3 cup milk

   2 tablespoons minced fresh parsley
1/4 teaspoon salt
1/2 cup shredded cheddar cheese

In a skillet, brown and crumble sausage until fully cooked. Remove sausage, reserving drippings. In the drippings, cook potatoes and onion until potatoes are browned, stirring occasionally. In a bowl, beat eggs, milk, parsley and salt; pour over potato mixture. Add sausage; cook and stir gently over medium heat until eggs are set. Sprinkle with cheese. Cover for 1-2 minutes or until cheese melts. **Yield:** 4 servings.

MEXICAN OMELET

Helen Sharp, Wiley, Colorado

Through the years, my family has enjoyed this tasty omelet for brunch. Now, as a 71-year-old farm wife, I often prepare it for friends when we gather for our many "senior" functions.

   1 flour tortilla (7 inches), coarsely chopped
2 tablespoons butter *or* margarine
8 eggs
1 tablespoon water
1/4 teaspoon salt
   1 cup (4 ounces) shredded Monterey Jack cheese, *divided*
1 large ripe avocado, chopped
3/4 cup sour cream, *divided*
3 tablespoons chopped fresh *or* canned green chilies
1 tablespoon lemon juice
1 medium tomato, chopped

In an 8-in. skillet, saute tortilla in butter until softened, about 2 minutes. Meanwhile, beat eggs, water and salt in a bowl. Pour over tortilla in skillet; cook over medium heat. As eggs set, lift edges, letting uncooked portion flow underneath. When eggs are set, remove from the heat. Sprinkle with 3/4 cup cheese. Combine avocado, 1/2 cup sour cream, chilies and lemon juice; spread over half of the omelet. Fold omelet in half and transfer to a warm platter. Top with tomato and remaining cheese and sour cream. **Yield:** 4 servings.

SOUTH-OF-THE-BORDER SCRAMBLED EGGS

Fay Dear, Glendive, Montana

When my family gathers at our cabin, these slightly spicy eggs are a must. And my kids insist I'm the only one who can make them. The crushed tortilla chips really add a unique but tasty texture.

   6 eggs
1/4 cup milk
3/4 cup crushed tortilla chips
3/4 cup chopped fully cooked ham
1/4 cup chopped onion

1/4 cup chopped green pepper
1 tablespoon butter *or* margarine
3/4 cup shredded cheddar cheese
1 small tomato, chopped
1/2 cup sour cream
Taco sauce

Lightly beat eggs with milk; add tortilla chips. Let stand for 15 minutes. In a large skillet, saute ham, onion and green pepper in butter. Add egg mixture and cook over medium heat, stirring occasionally, until eggs are set. Remove from the heat; gently stir in cheese and tomato. Serve in the skillet or transfer to a warm serving platter. Top with sour cream and taco sauce. **Yield:** 4 servings.

CHEESY HERBED EGGS

Ruth Sayles, Pendleton, Oregon

These scrambled eggs are one of the many hearty meals my family would enjoy before heading out to begin daily chores on the farm. The combination of herbs and cheeses gives basic eggs a flavorful taste.

1-1/3 cups light cream
1 teaspoon grated lemon peel
16 eggs, lightly beaten
1 teaspoon salt
1/2 teaspoon white pepper
1/4 teaspoon dried basil
1/4 teaspoon dried oregano
1/4 teaspoon crushed dried rosemary
1/2 cup shredded cheddar cheese
1/2 cup grated Parmesan cheese
1/4 cup butter *or* margarine
Tomato wedges, optional

In a large bowl, combine cream and lemon peel. Add eggs and seasonings; mix well. Stir in cheeses. In a large skillet, melt butter; pour in egg mixture. Cook and stir gently over medium heat until eggs are set, about 15 minutes. Garnish with tomato wedges if desired. **Yield:** 6-8 servings.

MY HUSBAND'S FAVORITE OMELET

Mary Bitterman, Willow Street, Pennsylvania

My husband asks me to serve this super-easy omelet at least once a week. As you can imagine, during our more than 40 years of marriage, I've made this dish too many times to count!

3 eggs
1/2 cup milk
3 tablespoons finely chopped onion
3 tablespoons finely chopped celery
3 tablespoons finely chopped broccoli
2 tablespoons chopped carrot
2 tablespoons chopped pimientos
3 bacon strips, cooked and crumbled
1/2 teaspoon salt
1/4 teaspoon pepper

1 tablespoon butter *or* margarine
4 thin slices process American cheese

Beat eggs with milk just until combined. Stir in vegetables, bacon, salt and pepper. In a medium skillet, heat butter until it sizzles; turn pan to coat bottom and sides. Add egg mixture; cook over medium heat. As eggs set, lift edges, letting uncooked portion flow underneath. When eggs are set, transfer to a warm platter and top with cheese. **Yield:** 1-2 servings.

EGG AND SAUSAGE POCKETS

Rita Addicks, Weimar, Texas

When I want to spice up my breakfast, I make these finger-licking, family-approved sausage sandwiches. They can be prepared quickly when I'm short on time. And it's a fun way to combine sausage and scrambled eggs.

1/4 pound bulk pork sausage
4 large *or* 8 small pita breads
3 green onions, sliced
1/2 teaspoon chili powder
6 eggs, lightly beaten

In a skillet, brown and crumble sausage until fully cooked. Meanwhile, cut pita breads in half crosswise; wrap in foil and warm in the oven. Drain fat from skillet; to sausage, add onions, chili powder and eggs. Cook and stir gently over medium heat until eggs are set. Spoon into pita halves. **Yield:** 4 servings.

BREAKFAST BURRITOS

Donna Poppe, Colfax, Illinois

When my family is in the mood for Mexican food, this is the recipe I reach for. It's a nice change of pace from traditional breakfast food. Your family will love the zippy flavor.

1 pound bulk pork sausage
12 eggs, lightly beaten
10 flour tortillas (7 inches), warmed
2 cups (16 ounces) sour cream
1 jar (16 ounces) picante sauce
1 can (2-1/4 ounces) sliced ripe olives, optional

In a large skillet, brown and crumble sausage; drain. Add eggs and cook over medium heat for 5-7 minutes or until set. Spoon about 1/4 cup egg mixture down center of each tortilla. Top each with sour cream, picante sauce and olives if desired. Fold in sides of tortilla. **Yield:** 6-8 servings.

ONE-PAN BREAKFAST

Nancy Block, Kansas City, Missouri
(PICTURED AT RIGHT)

Once when we had overnight guests, my husband, Ernie, made this easy all-in-one breakfast. It was a success. Now those guests request this dish whenever they come to visit.

    1 pound bulk pork sausage
    4 large potatoes, peeled, cooked and cubed
    1 large onion, chopped
    6 eggs, beaten
    6 slices process American cheese
Salt and pepper to taste

In a large skillet, brown and crumble sausage; add potatoes and onion. Cook over medium-high heat for 18-20 minutes or until potatoes are browned. Gradually stir in eggs; cook and stir until set. Remove from the heat; top with cheese. Season with salt and pepper. **Yield:** 4-6 servings.

CABIN HASH

Mrs. Lyman Hein, Rochester, Minnesota
(PICTURED AT RIGHT)

My family named this dish because I served it when we vacationed at our cabin on the Mississippi River. Now it's become such a favorite that I often make it when we're home.

  12 medium potatoes (about 4 pounds), peeled, cooked and cubed
   3 cups cubed fully cooked ham (about 1 pound)
1/2 cup chopped onion
1/2 cup butter *or* margarine
   1 package (10 ounces) frozen chopped broccoli, thawed
Salt and pepper to taste
Sour cream, optional

In a large skillet, cook potatoes, ham and onion in butter, stirring frequently, until potatoes are lightly browned. Add broccoli; heat through. Season with salt and pepper. Serve with sour cream if desired. **Yield:** 8-10 servings.

HASH BROWN OMELET

Carolyn McMasters, Jacksonville, Florida
(PICTURED AT RIGHT)

One of my favorite pastimes is cooking. My friends and family have always encouraged me...mainly because they get to sample my "creations". This recipe is a classic that I've been making for years.

    4 bacon strips
    2 cups frozen shredded hash brown potatoes
1/4 cup chopped onion
1/4 cup chopped green pepper
    4 eggs, lightly beaten
1/4 cup milk

    1/2 teaspoon salt
Dash pepper
    1 cup (4 ounces) shredded sharp cheddar cheese

In a medium nonstick skillet, cook bacon until crisp. Remove bacon; crumble and set aside. Add potatoes, onion and green pepper to drippings. Cook and stir over medium heat for 7-10 minutes or until potatoes are browned and vegetables are tender. In a bowl, beat eggs, milk, salt and pepper; pour over potatoes. Sprinkle with cheese and bacon. Cover and cook over medium-low heat for 10-15 minutes or until eggs are set. Do not stir. Fold in half. **Yield:** 2-3 servings.

FAST AND FLAVORFUL EGGS

Michele Christman, Sidney, Illinois

With a small ingredient list and short cooking time, this delicious recipe is one of my favorites. And with two toddlers vying for my attention, I need all the free time I can get!

    1/4 cup chopped green pepper
    1 tablespoon butter *or* margarine
    6 eggs, lightly beaten
    1 can (10-3/4 ounces) condensed cream of chicken soup, undiluted, *divided*
3/4 teaspoon salt
1/2 teaspoon pepper
    6 bacon strips, cooked and crumbled
1/2 cup milk

In a skillet, saute green pepper in butter until tender. Combine eggs, 1/2 cup soup, salt and pepper. Add to skillet; cook and stir gently until the eggs are set. Stir in bacon. For sauce, heat milk and remaining soup; stir until smooth. Serve over eggs. **Yield:** 3-4 servings.

FRIED CORNMEAL MUSH

Amanda Miller, Millersburg, Ohio

I've been eating cornmeal mush ever since I was a little girl. Now it's become popular with my family. I especially love this version because the batter is made ahead of time and fried the next morning.

    4 cups water, *divided*
    1 cup cornmeal
    1 teaspoon salt
Maple syrup

Boil 3 cups water. Combine remaining water with cornmeal and salt; add to boiling water. Stir until mixture returns to a boil. Reduce heat; cover and simmer for 1 hour, stirring occasionally. Pour into a greased 8-1/2-in. x 4-1/2-in. x 2-1/2-in. loaf pan. Chill for 8 hours or overnight. Slice 1/2 in. thick. Fry in a greased skillet until browned on each side. Serve with syrup. **Yield:** 14-16 servings.

> **JOLLY GOOD...ANYTIME!** *Pictured at right, clockwise from top left: One-Pan Breakfast, Hash Brown Omelet and Cabin Hash (all recipes on this page).*

MUSHROOM OMELET

Christine Walker, Oklawaha, Florida

This tasty variation of a basic omelet reminds me of my childhood when I'd help my father search for mushrooms in the forest near our home. The caraway seed really enhances the flavor of the mushrooms.

  1 tablespoon butter *or* margarine
  4 medium fresh mushrooms, sliced
  1/8 teaspoon caraway seed
  1/8 teaspoon lemon pepper
  3 eggs
  2 tablespoons milk
  1/8 teaspoon salt
Dash pepper

In an 8-in. skillet, heat butter until it sizzles. Saute mushrooms, caraway and lemon pepper for 3-5 minutes. In a small bowl, beat eggs, milk, salt and pepper. Pour over mushrooms. Cook over medium heat. As eggs set, lift edges, letting uncooked portion flow underneath. When eggs are set, fold omelet in half. **Yield:** 1-2 servings.

COUNTRY SAUSAGE GRAVY

June Smith, Byron Center, Michigan

The men in my family love this truly country breakfast dish because of its hearty flavor. I love it because it's so easy to make.

  1 pound bulk pork sausage
  1 can (10-3/4 ounces) condensed cream of
    chicken soup, undiluted
  1 soup can milk
  1/2 teaspoon dry mustard
  1/4 teaspoon seasoned salt
  1/4 teaspoon pepper
  1 cup (8 ounces) sour cream
Warm biscuits

In a heavy skillet, brown and crumble sausage over medium heat until fully cooked. Drain and set aside. In the same skillet, combine soup and milk. Add mustard, seasoned salt and pepper; bring to a boil. Reduce heat. Add sausage and sour cream. Simmer until heated through (do not boil). Serve over warm biscuits. **Yield:** 4-6 servings (3-1/2 cups gravy).

GARDEN FRESH BREAKFAST

Donna King, Stewartsville, Missouri

Here in northwest Missouri, we have an abundance of zucchini, peppers, onions and tomatoes. So I make this attractive garden recipe a lot, and that pleases my hungry family!

  8 ounces fresh mushrooms, sliced
  1 cup chopped zucchini
  1/2 cup chopped green pepper
  1/4 cup sliced green onions

  2 tablespoons butter *or* margarine
  1 medium tomato, diced and seeded
  4 eggs
  2 tablespoons water
  2 tablespoons Dijon mustard
  1/2 teaspoon salt
  1/4 teaspoon pepper
  1 cup (4 ounces) shredded Monterey Jack cheese
Paprika

In a large skillet, saute mushrooms, zucchini, green pepper and onions in butter for 5 minutes or until tender. Drain off juices. Stir in tomato. In a bowl, beat the eggs, water, mustard, salt and pepper. Pour over vegetables. Cover and cook over medium heat for 5-10 minutes or until eggs are set. Sprinkle with cheese and paprika. Cut into wedges to serve. **Yield:** 4-6 servings.

CREAMED HAM AND EGGS

Karen Falb, Columbiana, Ohio

When I got married, my husband asked me to get this favorite recipe from his mother. I like to serve it with homemade bran muffins and applesauce.

  3 tablespoons butter *or* margarine
  1/4 cup all-purpose flour
  1/2 teaspoon dry mustard
  1/8 teaspoon pepper
  2 cups milk
  1/2 teaspoon Worcestershire sauce
  3 hard-cooked eggs, diced
  2 cups cubed fully cooked ham
  3 slices toast, cut into triangles

In a saucepan, melt butter. Add flour, mustard and pepper; cook until bubbly. Gradually add milk and Worcestershire sauce; cook and stir until thickened. Stir in eggs and ham; heat through. Serve hot over toast. **Yield:** 2-3 servings.

CANADIAN BACON BREAKFAST

Doris Heath, Bryson City, North Carolina

These pretty puffs are not only a complete breakfast in one, they're also an attractive addition to your breakfast table.

  6 tablespoons Dijon mustard
  6 tablespoons honey
  6 English muffins, split and toasted
  2 tablespoons butter *or* margarine
  12 slices Canadian bacon *or* thinly sliced ham
  1 large Granny Smith apple, peeled and
    thinly sliced
  5 egg whites
  1 cup (4 ounces) shredded cheddar cheese
  1/2 teaspoon paprika

Combine mustard and honey; spread 1 tablespoon on each muffin half. In a large skillet, melt butter. Add Canadian bacon and heat through; remove to paper towels to drain. Cook apple slices in the drippings until tender. Arrange bacon on muffins; top with apple slices. Place on a baking sheet. In a mixing bowl, beat egg whites until stiff peaks form. Fold in cheese and paprika; spread over apples. Broil muffins until puffed and golden. **Yield:** 6 servings.

MARLENE'S HASH BROWN SUPREME

Marlene Peterson, Kimball, Minnesota

As a cook in a restaurant, I'm always searching for new recipes. One day I came up with this new breakfast item and served it to some of our "regulars". They declared it a success, and it has since been added to the menu.

    3 tablespoons butter *or* margarine
    3/4 cup frozen cubed hash brown potatoes
    1/3 cup diced onion
    1/3 cup diced green pepper
    1/3 cup diced tomato
    1/3 cup sliced fresh mushrooms
    1/2 cup diced fully cooked ham
Salt and pepper to taste
    1/2 cup shredded Swiss cheese

In a medium nonstick skillet, melt butter. Add the next six ingredients; mix well. Cook over medium-high heat for 10-15 minutes, stirring occasionally, or until potatoes are browned. Season with salt and pepper. Sprinkle with cheese. Cover and cook over low heat for 2 minutes longer or until cheese is melted. **Yield:** 1-2 servings.

SOUTHWEST SKILLET DISH

Virginia Varner, Tucson, Arizona

My family and friends love this variation of plain fried potatoes because they add some "zing" to our breakfast. And for even more Southwestern flair, we top ours with my homemade salsa.

    4 tablespoons butter *or* margarine
    5 to 6 cups thinly sliced peeled raw potatoes
    6 slices fully cooked ham, cubed
    1 can (4 ounces) chopped green chilies
    1 cup (4 ounces) shredded Colby cheese
Salsa

In a 10-in. cast-iron skillet, melt butter over medium heat. Fry potatoes until lightly browned and tender. Add ham and cook until heated through. Sprinkle with chilies and cheese. Remove from the heat and cover until the cheese is melted. Serve in the skillet. Top with salsa. **Yield:** 4-6 servings.

NEW ORLEANS BRUNCH EGGS

Cindy Sandine, Oklahoma City, Oklahoma

My husband and I don't have any family nearby, so we often invite friends over for special weekend brunches. Of all the dishes I serve, guests seem to like this the best.

    1/2 cup finely chopped fresh mushrooms
    1/2 cup finely chopped fully cooked ham
    1/2 cup finely chopped green onions

    2 garlic cloves, minced
    2 tablespoons butter *or* margarine
    2 tablespoons all-purpose flour
    1/8 teaspoon cayenne pepper
1-1/4 cups beef broth
    8 slices grilled ham
    8 eggs, poached
    4 English muffins, split and toasted

In a skillet, saute mushrooms, chopped ham, onions and garlic in butter until vegetables are tender. Stir in flour and cayenne pepper. Blend in broth; simmer, stirring occasionally, for 20 minutes. To serve, place a slice of ham and an egg on each muffin half. Spoon sauce over each. **Yield:** 4-6 servings.

BACON-POTATO BURRITOS

Reesa Byrd, Enterprise, Alabama

I've been cooking for some 45 years. So to keep my interest in the kitchen, I like to try new recipes. You'll enjoy the tasty, hearty flavor of these unique breakfast burritos.

    8 bacon strips
1-1/2 cups frozen Southern-style hash brown
      potatoes
    2 teaspoons minced dried onion
    4 eggs
    1/4 cup milk
    1 teaspoon Worcestershire sauce
    1/4 teaspoon salt
    1/4 teaspoon pepper
    1 cup (4 ounces) shredded cheddar cheese
    6 flour tortillas (7 inches)
Salsa

In a large skillet, cook bacon until crisp; drain on paper towels. Brown potatoes and onion in drippings. In a bowl, beat eggs; add milk, Worcestershire sauce, salt and pepper. Pour over potatoes; cook and stir until eggs are set. Crumble bacon and stir into eggs. Sprinkle with cheese. Meanwhile, warm tortillas according to package directions. Spoon egg mixture down center of tortillas; fold in sides of tortilla. Serve with salsa. **Yield:** 4-6 servings.

HOT JAM BREAKFAST SANDWICHES

Gloria Jarrett, Loveland, Ohio

These slightly sweet sandwiches give a whole new meaning to grilled sandwiches. The combination of flavors are guaranteed to appeal to everyone.

    1/4 cup butter *or* margarine, softened
    1/4 cup flaked coconut
    1/2 cup apricot jam
    1/2 teaspoon ground cinnamon
    12 slices raisin bread

In a bowl, mix butter and coconut; stir in jam and cinnamon. Spread between slices of bread. Grill on a greased skillet until golden brown on both sides. **Yield:** 6 servings.

FRIED SAUSAGE GRITS

Kay Goldman, Punta Gorda, Florida
(PICTURED AT LEFT)

My mother used to make a version of this recipe using hominy and salmon. One day I substituted sausage and grits and decided I liked it better than the original.

   4 cups water
   1 teaspoon salt
   1 cup quick-cooking grits
1/2 pound bulk pork sausage
   1 small onion, finely chopped
Cornmeal

In a saucepan, bring water and salt to a boil; slowly add grits, stirring constantly. Reduce heat to medium-low; cover and cook for 5-7 minutes or until very thick; set aside. In a skillet, cook and crumble sausage until browned; drain. Add sausage and onion to grits; mix well. Spoon into a greased 8-1/2-in. x 4-1/2-in. x 2-1/2-in. loaf pan. Chill overnight. Remove from pan; cut into 1/2-in. slices. Roll slices in cornmeal. Cook in a greased skillet until golden brown on both sides. **Yield:** 6-8 servings.

SKIER'S SKILLET

Lynn Cronk, Indianapolis, Indiana
(PICTURED AT LEFT)

With its great combination of flavors and ease of preparation, this is one of my favorite dishes to make when we have overnight guests. Serve it with scrambled eggs for a complete meal...with little fuss!

   1 package (12 ounces) pork sausage links
   5 medium apples (about 1-1/4 pounds), peeled and quartered
   3 tablespoons brown sugar
   1 tablespoon lemon juice
1/8 teaspoon salt

In a 10-in. skillet over medium-high heat, cook sausages for 10 minutes, turning occasionally; drain. Add apple wedges. Sprinkle with brown sugar, lemon juice and salt. Cover and cook over medium heat for 10-15 minutes or until apples are tender and sausages are fully cooked. **Yield:** 6 servings.

BREAKFAST MESS

Dee Anderson, Kent, Washington
(PICTURED AT LEFT)

Whenever my family goes camping (which is a lot!), this wonderful filling breakfast really gets the day going. Everyone who's tried this "Anderson Family Special" agrees that it's the best.

WINTER WARM-UPS. *Pictured at left, top to bottom: Fried Sausage Grits, Breakfast Mess and Skier's Skillet (all recipes on this page).*

---

   1 package (26 ounces) frozen shredded hash brown potatoes
1/4 cup cooking oil
   1 large green pepper, chopped
   1 large onion, chopped
   2 garlic cloves, minced
   2 cans (12 ounces *each*) Spam, cubed *or* 3 cups cubed fully cooked ham
   6 eggs, lightly beaten
1/2 teaspoon salt
1/4 teaspoon pepper
1-1/2 cups (6 ounces) shredded cheddar cheese

In a large skillet, fry potatoes in oil for 10 minutes. Add green pepper, onion and garlic; continue to cook for 25 minutes or until potatoes are browned and vegetables are tender. Stir in Spam; heat through. Cover and remove from the heat. In another greased skillet, combine eggs, salt and pepper. Cook and stir gently until eggs are set. Stir into potato mixture. Top with cheese; cover for 3-5 minutes or until cheese is melted. **Yield:** 6-8 servings.

GET MORE FOR YOUR CLUCK. *You can increase the volume of scrambled eggs by removing the eggs from the refrigerator 30 minutes before beating.*

EGG FOO YUNG BREAKFAST

Mary Jo Amos, Noel, Missouri

This recipe proves that "the most important meal of the day" doesn't have to be boring! Not only is this unique dish delicious, it adds a festive look to your breakfast table.

   1 cup cooked white rice
1/4 cup chopped onion
   1 teaspoon soy sauce
1/2 teaspoon dried parsley flakes
1/2 teaspoon sugar
1/2 teaspoon salt
1/4 teaspoon ground ginger
   2 eggs, lightly beaten
1/2 cup frozen peas
   1 tablespoon butter *or* margarine
SAUCE:
   1 cup water
   1 tablespoon cornstarch
   1 package (3 ounces) Oriental-flavor ramen noodle soup mix with seasoning packet

In a large bowl, combine rice, onion, soy sauce, parsley, sugar, salt and ginger; mix well. Stir in eggs and peas. Carefully shape mixture into four patties. In a skillet, melt butter over medium heat. Brown patties on both sides, about 5 minutes total. Meanwhile, in a saucepan, bring water, cornstarch and seasoning packet to a boil. Reduce heat to low; add noodles. Cook and stir for about 5 minutes. Serve over patties. **Yield:** 4 servings.

Cookin' Up...
PANCAKES, WAFFLES & FRENCH TOAST

Dripping with sweet and sticky toppings, these hot-off-the-griddle goodies are guaranteed to wake up your family's tired taste buds.

FRUIT-TOPPED BLINTZES

Patricia Larsen, Thayne, Wyoming
(PICTURED AT LEFT)

My mother is a wonderful cook who always likes to prepare (and improve on!) dishes she's sampled at restaurants. That's what I did with these blintzes, and my family loves my fruity version even more than the original.

BLINTZES:
    9 eggs
    1 cup all-purpose flour
    1/4 cup cornstarch
    1/8 teaspoon salt
    3 cups milk
FILLING:
    2 packages (8 ounces *each*) cream cheese, softened
    1/2 cup confectioners' sugar
Pureed raspberries *or* strawberries
Whipped cream, optional
Fresh raspberries *or* strawberries, optional

In a bowl, beat eggs. Add flour, cornstarch and salt; stir until smooth. Stir in milk. Pour 1/3 cup batter into a lightly greased hot 8-in. skillet. Cook over medium heat until set and lightly browned. Turn and cook for 1 minute. Keep in a warm oven, covered with paper towels. Repeat with remaining batter. For filling, beat cream cheese and confectioners' sugar in a mixing bowl. Place about 2 tablespoons in the center of each blintz; overlap sides and ends on top of filling. Place folded side down. Top with pureed berries; garnish with whipped cream and fresh berries if desired. **Yield:** 6-8 servings.

FRENCH TOAST SUPREME

Janis Hoople, Stanton, Michigan
(PICTURED AT LEFT)

As teachers, my husband and I rarely have time for breakfast during the week. So we look forward to relax-

SWEET TREATS. *Pictured at left, clockwise from the bottom: Fruit-Topped Blintzes, French Toast Supreme and Waffles with Vanilla Sauce (all recipes on this page).*

ing breakfasts with our daughters on weekends. The cinnamon bread in this recipe is a nice variation.

    3 eggs
    1/4 cup milk
    1 tablespoon sugar
    1 teaspoon vanilla extract
    1 carton (4 ounces) whipped cream cheese
    12 slices cinnamon bread
Kiwifruit and starfruit, optional

In a bowl, beat eggs, milk, sugar and vanilla. Spread 1 tablespoon cream cheese on six slices of bread; top with remaining slices to make six sandwiches. Dip sandwiches in egg mixture. Fry on a lightly greased skillet until golden brown on both sides. Garnish with kiwi and starfruit if desired. **Yield:** 4-6 servings.

WAFFLES WITH VANILLA SAUCE

Sandra Falk, Steinbach, Manitoba
(PICTURED AT LEFT)

I like to serve these flavorful waffles when we have company because they add nice color to the table and look so elegant, yet they're so easy to prepare. Everyone raves about the unique rich vanilla sauce served over the warm waffles.

    1-2/3 cups all-purpose flour
    4 teaspoons baking powder
    1/2 teaspoon salt
    2 eggs, *separated*
    3-2/3 cups milk, *divided*
    6 tablespoons vegetable oil
    1/2 cup sugar
    1 teaspoon vanilla extract
Fresh strawberries

In a bowl, combine flour, baking powder and salt. In another bowl, beat egg yolks lightly. Add 1-2/3 cups milk and oil; stir into dry ingredients just until moistened. Set aside 1/4 cup batter in a small bowl. Beat egg whites until stiff peaks form; fold into remaining batter. Bake in a preheated waffle iron according to manufacturer's directions until golden brown. In a saucepan, heat sugar and remaining milk until scalded. Stir a small amount into reserved batter; return all to pan. Bring to a boil; boil for 5-7 minutes or until thickened. Remove from the heat; add vanilla and mix well (sauce will thicken upon standing). Serve over waffles. Top with berries. **Yield:** 6-8 waffles (6-1/2 inches).

BREAKFAST PUDDING CREPES

Sue Gronholz, Columbus, Wisconsin

This originally was a dessert recipe, but my family enjoyed it so much that I turned it into a breakfast meal. Served with bacon or sausage, these tasty treats are a "crepe" way to start the day!

    1 cup biscuit mix
    1 cup milk
    2 eggs
FILLING:
    1 package (3.4 ounces) instant French vanilla
      pudding mix
    2 cups cold milk
    1 cup whipped topping
    1 pint fresh strawberries, sliced *or* 1 can
      (21 ounces) blueberry *or* cherry pie filling
Additional whipped topping and strawberries *or*
  pie filling, optional

In a mixing bowl, beat biscuit mix, milk and eggs until smooth. Heat a lightly greased 8-in. skillet; add 3 tablespoons batter, lift and turn pan to cover bottom. Cook until lightly browned; turn and brown the other side. Repeat with remaining batter, greasing skillet as needed. Stack crepes with waxed paper between layers. For filling, in a small mixing bowl, beat pudding mix and milk for 1 minute. Add whipped topping; beat for 1 minute. Place about 3 tablespoons of fruit or pie filling down the center of each crepe. Top with about 1/4 cup pudding mixture. Roll up crepes and place on a serving platter. If desired, top each crepe with additional whipped topping and fruit or pie filling. **Yield:** about 12 crepes.

PERFECT PANCAKES. *Turn pancakes as soon as they puff up and fill with bubbles. If you wait for the bubbles to break, the pancakes will be tough.*

ZUCCHINI POTATO PANCAKES

Gabriele Hoover, Salem, West Virginia

Living on a 90-acre farm, I've learned to love gardening and canning. I freeze lots of zucchini already measured out for this recipe. With my family of five, I can never get away with making just one batch of these delicious pancakes!

    2 medium zucchini, coarsely grated (about 1-1/2
      cups)
    1 large potato, peeled and finely shredded (about
      1-1/4 cups)
    1 small onion, grated
    2 tablespoons cornmeal
    2 tablespoons all-purpose flour
  3/4 teaspoon salt
    1 egg, lightly beaten

Cooking oil
Sour cream

In a sieve or colander, drain zucchini, squeezing to remove excess liquid. Place zucchini in a mixing bowl; add potato and onion. Stir in cornmeal, flour, salt and egg; mix well. Coat the bottom of a skillet with oil. Add 2 tablespoons batter. Press lightly to flatten. Cook over medium heat until golden brown, about 3-4 minutes on each side. Repeat with remaining batter. Serve with sour cream. **Yield:** 16 pancakes.

APPLESAUCE/SAUSAGE WAFFLES

Kathy Waldo, Southington, Ohio

I can remember my mother preparing these hearty "meal-in-one" waffles when I was growing up. Now I often make them for my own clan using eggs from our chickens, and homemade sausage and applesauce.

      1 pound bulk pork sausage
  2-1/2 cups all-purpose flour
      4 teaspoons baking powder
      1 teaspoon ground cinnamon
    1/8 teaspoon ground nutmeg
      3 eggs, *separated*
  1-1/3 cups milk
      1 cup applesauce
    2/3 cup vegetable oil

In a skillet, brown and crumble sausage until no longer pink. Meanwhile, in a large bowl, combine flour, baking powder, cinnamon and nutmeg. In another bowl, beat egg yolks lightly. Add milk, applesauce and oil; mix well. Stir into dry ingredients just until combined. Beat egg whites until stiff peaks form; fold into batter. Drain sausage; add to batter. Bake in a preheated waffle iron according to manufacturer's directions until golden brown. **Yield:** 8 waffles (about 6-1/2 inches).

VIENNESE PANCAKES

Ruth Stenson, Santa Ana, California

This is one of the many recipes passed down through my family. These light and lemony pancakes take some time to prepare, but your family will show their appreciation with sounds of "Mmmm!" and happy faces!

    2/3 cup all-purpose flour
    1/2 cup milk
    1/3 cup water
      1 egg
    1/8 teaspoon salt
FILLING:
      1 package (8 ounces) cream cheese, softened
      6 tablespoons sugar
      2 eggs, *separated*
    1/4 cup raisins, chopped
    1/4 cup sliced almonds
      1 teaspoon grated lemon peel
    1/8 teaspoon salt
      2 teaspoons brown sugar
Additional sliced almonds, optional

In a mixing bowl, combine flour, milk, water, egg and salt; beat until smooth. Cover and let stand for 1 hour. In a lightly greased 8-in. skillet over medium-high heat, add 2-3 tablespoons batter; lift and tilt skillet to cover bottom. Cook until lightly browned; turn and brown the other side. Repeat with remaining batter, greasing skillet as needed. Stack pancakes with waxed paper between layers. For filling, beat cream cheese and sugar in a mixing bowl until light and fluffy. Beat in egg yolks. Stir in raisins, almonds, lemon peel and salt. Place 1 tablespoon filling down the center of each pancake; set remaining filling aside. Roll up pancakes and place seam side down in a greased 12-in. x 8-in. x 2-in. baking dish. In a small bowl, beat egg whites until stiff; fold in reserved filling. Spoon over pancakes; sprinkle with brown sugar and almonds if desired. Bake, uncovered, at 350° for 20-25 minutes or until edges are lightly browned. **Yield:** about 13 pancakes.

PUFFED EGGNOG PANCAKE
Nancy Callis, Woodinville, Washington

This is a tasty breakfast that I love to make at Christmas. I pop the pancake in the oven while the family opens gifts.

  2 tablespoons butter *or* margarine
  3 eggs
2/3 cup eggnog
1/2 cup all-purpose flour
1/4 cup sliced almonds
  2 teaspoons sugar

Place butter in a 10-in. cast-iron skillet; place in a 425° oven for 2-3 minutes or until melted. In a mixing bowl, beat eggs until fluffy. Add eggnog and flour; beat until smooth. Pour into hot skillet. Sprinkle with almonds and sugar. Bake for 16-18 minutes or until puffed and browned. Serve immediately. **Yield:** 4-6 servings.

BACON WAFFLES
Mrs. Phillip Hatcher, Sand Springs, Oklahoma

My husband saw these appealing waffles on a television cooking show and decided to try them himself. The whole family enjoyed the combination of flavors, and I enjoyed the time off from cooking!

  1 pound sliced bacon
1-3/4 cups all-purpose flour
  1 tablespoon sugar
  2 teaspoons baking powder
1/2 teaspoon salt
  3 eggs, *separated*
1-1/2 cups milk
1/4 cup butter *or* margarine, melted

In a skillet, cook bacon until crisp. Drain; crumble and set aside. In a mixing bowl, combine the flour, sugar, baking powder and salt. Beat egg yolks, milk and butter; stir into dry ingredients until smooth. Beat egg whites until stiff peaks form; fold into batter. Add bacon. Before making each waffle, stir batter. Bake in a preheated waffle iron according to manufacturer's directions until golden brown. **Yield:** 8-10 waffles (about 6-3/4 inches).

HONEY-BAKED FRENCH TOAST
Charlene Berg, Osceola, Wisconsin

A few years ago, my husband and I opened a bed-and-breakfast on our century-old dairy farm. Our guests always look forward to our hearty country breakfasts like this French toast.

  3 eggs
  4 tablespoons honey, *divided*
1-1/2 teaspoons ground cinnamon
  1 cup milk
15 slices day-old French bread (cut diagonally 3/4 inch thick)
  3 tablespoons brown sugar
  2 tablespoons butter *or* margarine, melted
Maple syrup

In a bowl, beat eggs with 2 tablespoons honey and cinnamon; stir in milk. Dip bread into egg mixture. In a greased 13-in. x 9-in. x 2-in. baking pan, arrange three rows of five slices of bread, overlapping slices slightly. Cover and chill 8 hours or overnight. Remove from refrigerator 30 minutes before baking. Sprinkle brown sugar over bread; drizzle with butter and remaining honey. Bake at 350° for 30 minutes. Serve with syrup. **Yield:** 6-8 servings.

WORLD'S BEST WAFFLES
Judy Lichti, Shickley, Nebraska

I pride myself as being a good cook who learned everything about baking and cooking from my very patient mother. Credit also goes to my father, who suffered through my many less-than-successful experiments!

  1 package (1/4 ounce) active dry yeast
  1 tablespoon sugar
  2 cups warm milk (110° to 115°)
  4 eggs, *separated*
  1 teaspoon vanilla extract
2-1/2 cups all-purpose flour
1/2 teaspoon salt
1/4 teaspoon ground nutmeg
1/2 cup butter *or* margarine, melted

In a mixing bowl, dissolve yeast and sugar in warm milk. Beat egg yolks lightly; add to yeast mixture with vanilla. Combine flour, salt and nutmeg; stir into yeast mixture just until combined. Add butter; mix well. Beat egg whites until stiff peaks form; fold into batter. Cover and let rise until doubled, about 45-60 minutes. Bake in a preheated waffle iron according to manufacturer's directions until golden brown. **Yield:** 12-16 waffles (about 6-1/2 inches).

RISE-AND-SHINE BREAKFASTS. *Clockwise from bottom left: Cornmeal Hotcakes, Oatmeal Nut Waffles, Apple-Pear Puff Pancake, Strawberry-Banana French Toast and Old-Fashioned Potato Pancakes (all recipes on page 40).*

OLD-FASHIONED POTATO PANCAKES

LeeAnn Greff, Minot, North Dakota
(PICTURED ON PAGE 39)

If you're looking for a change of pace for breakfast, try these old-fashioned potato pancakes. They were my grandmother's favorite breakfast dish, and the recipe has been passed down through the generations.

>   3 cups shredded peeled potatoes
>   2 eggs, lightly beaten
> 1/4 cup grated onion
> 1/4 cup all-purpose flour
>   3 tablespoons minced fresh parsley
>   1 teaspoon salt
>   1 teaspoon pepper

Rinse potatoes in cold water; drain thoroughly. In a bowl, mix potatoes, eggs, onion, flour, parsley, salt and pepper. Pour batter by 1/3 cupfuls onto a greased hot griddle. Fry 5-6 minutes on each side or until potatoes are tender and pancakes are golden brown. **Yield:** 7-9 pancakes.

OATMEAL NUT WAFFLES

Joan Scott, Dunbar, Wisconsin
(PICTURED ON PAGE 38)

When I found this recipe in a church cookbook early in my marriage, I was eager to try it. It was an immediate success and has been a family favorite ever since. I even serve these hearty waffles for a different kind of supper.

> 1-1/2 cups whole wheat flour
>   2 teaspoons baking powder
> 1/2 teaspoon salt
>   2 eggs, lightly beaten
>   2 cups milk
> 1/4 cup butter *or* margarine, melted
>   2 tablespoons honey
>   1 cup quick-cooking oats
>   1 cup chopped nuts
> Sliced fresh peaches, optional

In a mixing bowl, combine flour, baking powder and salt. Combine eggs, milk, butter and honey; stir into dry ingredients and mix well. Fold in oats and nuts. Bake in a preheated waffle iron according to manufacturer's directions until golden brown. Garnish with peaches if desired. **Yield:** 8-10 waffles (about 6-3/4 inches).

CORNMEAL HOTCAKES

Jean Fogg, Rye, Colorado
(PICTURED ON PAGE 38)

My family loves the taste and texture of corn bread, so I knew I had to try this recipe. I hope your family enjoys these golden hotcakes as much as my family does!

> 1-1/2 cups yellow cornmeal
> 1/4 cup all-purpose flour
>   1 teaspoon baking soda

>   1 teaspoon sugar
>   1 teaspoon salt
>   2 cups buttermilk
>   2 tablespoons vegetable oil
>   1 egg, *separated*

In a mixing bowl, combine cornmeal, flour, baking soda, sugar and salt. In another bowl, beat buttermilk, oil and egg yolk; stir into dry ingredients. Beat egg white until stiff peaks form; fold into batter. Let stand 10 minutes. Pour batter by 1/4 cupfuls onto a lightly greased hot griddle; turn when bubbles form on top of pancakes. Cook until second side is golden brown. **Yield:** 16 pancakes.

APPLE-PEAR PUFF PANCAKE

Carol Williams, St. Joseph, Missouri
(PICTURED ON PAGE 39)

Whenever I serve this fruity puff pancake to family and friends, they think I slaved for hours in the kitchen. They're surprised to learn that such an attractive, delicious dish could be so easy to prepare.

>   3 tablespoons butter *or* margarine
>   4 eggs
>   1 cup milk
>   1 cup all-purpose flour
>   1 tablespoon sugar
> 1/8 teaspoon ground nutmeg
> **TOPPING:**
>   3 tablespoons butter *or* margarine
>   3 apples, sliced
>   3 pears, sliced
>   3 tablespoons sugar
> Maple syrup, optional

Place butter in a 10-in. ovenproof skillet; place in a 425° oven for 2-3 minutes or until melted. In a blender, process eggs, milk, flour, sugar and nutmeg until smooth. Pour into hot skillet. Bake for 20 minutes or until puffy. Meanwhile, for topping, melt butter in a large skillet. Cook apples, pears and sugar for 12-15 minutes or until fruit is tender, stirring occasionally. Pour over pancake and cut into wedges. Serve with syrup if desired. **Yield:** 4-6 servings.

STRAWBERRY-BANANA FRENCH TOAST

Marcella Perrigo, Bothell, Washington
(PICTURED ON PAGE 39)

My husband and I are avid cooks. In fact, we feel like most of our 30 years together have been spent in the kitchen! We've experimented with so many recipes, but this one remains at the top of our list.

>   10 to 12 slices day-old French bread (1 inch thick)
>   5 eggs, lightly beaten
> 3/4 cup milk
>   1 tablespoon vanilla extract
> 1/4 teaspoon baking powder
>   1 bag (16 ounces) frozen whole strawberries
>   4 firm bananas, sliced

1 cup sugar
1 tablespoon pumpkin pie *or* apple pie spice
1 tablespoon cinnamon-sugar

Place bread slices in a large shallow baking dish. Combine eggs, milk, vanilla and baking powder; pour over bread. Cover and chill 8 hours or overnight. Remove from refrigerator 30 minutes before baking. In a bowl, combine strawberries, bananas, sugar and pie spice; pour into a greased 13-in. x 9-in. x 2-in. baking dish. Arrange prepared bread on top. Sprinkle with cinnamon-sugar. Bake, uncovered, at 400° for 30-35 minutes. **Yield:** 6-8 servings.

BAKED FRENCH TOAST
WITH HOME-STYLE SYRUP

Deloris Asmus, Waseca, Minnesota

This variation of typical French toast is both simple to prepare and delicious. And the homemade syrup has more flavor than bottled pancake syrup ever could. I hope you like them both!

    4 eggs, lightly beaten
    1 cup milk
    2 teaspoons vanilla extract
    1 teaspoon salt
   12 slices day-old French bread (1/2 inch thick)
1-1/4 cups crushed cornflakes
    1 to 2 tablespoons butter *or* margarine
SYRUP:
1-1/2 cups sugar
  2/3 cup light corn syrup
  1/2 cup water
    1 teaspoon ground cinnamon
    1 can (5 ounces) evaporated milk
  1/2 teaspoon butter flavoring
  1/2 teaspoon almond extract

In a shallow dish or pie plate, combine eggs, milk, vanilla and salt. Add bread and soak for 5 minutes, turning once to coat. Coat each slice with cornflake crumbs and place on a well-greased baking sheet. Dot each slice with butter. Bake at 450° for 10-12 minutes or until golden brown. For syrup, combine sugar, corn syrup, water and cinnamon in a saucepan. Bring to a boil. Boil, stirring constantly, for 2 minutes. Remove from the heat; stir in evaporated milk and flavorings. Serve over warm French toast. **Yield:** 6-8 servings.

APPLE PANCAKE TIER

Ellen Govertsen, Wheaton, Illinois

When our two college-age sons come home, they request their favorite apple pancake recipe. I especially like to make it in the fall...after my husband and I have purchased our usual 4 bushels of apples!

    6 eggs
    1 cup milk
    1 cup all-purpose flour
  3/4 teaspoon salt
  1/2 teaspoon ground cinnamon

5 tablespoons butter *or* margarine, melted, *divided*
6 to 7 cups sliced peeled baking apples (about 2-1/2 pounds)
1/4 cup sugar
1 teaspoon grated lemon peel
Confectioners' sugar

In a mixing bowl, beat eggs until fluffy. Add milk. Combine flour, salt and cinnamon; add to egg mixture and mix well. Brush 3 tablespoons butter on sides and bottom of three 9-in. pie pans (using 1 tablespoon in each pan). Divide batter evenly between the pans. Bake at 400° for 20-25 minutes or until golden and puffy. Heat remaining butter in a skillet. Saute apples for 10 minutes or until crisp-tender. Stir in sugar and continue cooking for 5 minutes or until apples are tender. Drain, reserving juice. When pancakes are done, stack on a serving plate in this order: one pancake, a third of the apples and a third of the lemon peel. Repeat layers. Dust with confectioners' sugar. Pass reserved apple juice if desired. **Yield:** 6 servings.

MAPLE BUTTER

Carole Bilodeau, Kitchener, Ontario

My family loves the flavor of French toast in the morning. So for a little variety, we like to replace maple syrup with this slightly sweet topping.

3/4 cup butter *or* margarine, softened
1/2 cup maple syrup

In a mixing bowl, beat butter until smooth. Gradually add syrup, continuing to beat until smooth. Freeze in small portions. **Yield:** 1 cup.

ETHAN'S APPLE-NUT PANCAKES

Rene Laughlin, Woodland, California

I created this recipe so my son, Ethan, could get a nutritious breakfast. I was afraid he'd turn up his nose, but just one bite and he pronounced them yummy!

    2 cups all-purpose flour
  1/2 cup wheat germ
    2 teaspoons baking powder
    1 teaspoon baking soda
    1 teaspoon salt
    1 teaspoon ground cinnamon
    2 cups buttermilk
    2 eggs, lightly beaten
  1/2 cup applesauce
    1 tablespoon molasses
  1/2 cup chopped walnuts
    1 apple, peeled and grated

In a large mixing bowl, combine flour, wheat germ, baking powder, baking soda, salt and cinnamon. Combine buttermilk, eggs, applesauce and molasses; add to dry ingredients and mix well. Fold in walnuts and apple. Pour batter by 1/4 cupfuls onto a lightly greased hot griddle; turn when bubbles form on top of pancakes. Cook until second side is golden brown. **Yield:** 20-22 pancakes.

QUICK AND EASY WAFFLES

Phyllis McCosh, Abilene, Kansas

These fast-to-prepare waffles are perfect to whip up at the last minute, and the recipe can easily be doubled. I often made them when our six children were growing up. And now when they come back to visit, they always request them.

    2 cups biscuit mix
    2 eggs, lightly beaten
1/2 cup vegetable oil
    7 ounces lemon-lime soda

In a mixing bowl, combine biscuit mix, eggs and oil. Add soda and mix well. Bake in a preheated waffle iron according to manufacturer's directions until golden brown. **Yield:** 4-5 waffles (about 6-3/4 inches).

HONEY APPLE TOPPING

Kathi Jessee, Woodland, California

I'll admit it...I'm not a morning person. But I do look forward to spending time with family and preparing a special breakfast of homemade pancakes or waffles served with this tasty topping.

    2 tart apples, peeled and chopped
1/3 cup apple juice *or* cider
    2 tablespoons honey
1/8 teaspoon ground cinnamon

Combine all ingredients in a blender; process until smooth. Serve warm or cold over waffles or pancakes. **Yield:** 1-1/2 cups.

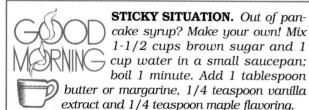

STICKY SITUATION. *Out of pancake syrup? Make your own! Mix 1-1/2 cups brown sugar and 1 cup water in a small saucepan; boil 1 minute. Add 1 tablespoon butter or margarine, 1/4 teaspoon vanilla extract and 1/4 teaspoon maple flavoring.*

APPLE-CINNAMON BAKED FRENCH TOAST

John Cashen, Moline, Illinois

When my wife and I hosted a breakfast for our church group, we wanted to avoid the last-minute rush of cooking. So we decided to try this make-ahead French toast. Everyone loved it and requested the recipe.

10 slices day-old French bread (3/4 inch thick)
    6 eggs, lightly beaten
2-3/4 cups milk
  2/3 cup sugar, *divided*
    1 tablespoon vanilla extract
    4 medium apples, peeled and thinly sliced

    2 teaspoons ground cinnamon
3/4 teaspoon ground nutmeg
    1 tablespoon butter *or* margarine

Place bread in a greased 13-in. x 9-in. x 2-in. baking dish. Combine eggs, milk, 1/3 cup sugar and vanilla; pour half over bread. Top with half of the apples. Combine cinnamon, nutmeg and remaining sugar; sprinkle half over apples. Top with the remaining apples. Pour remaining egg mixture over apples and sprinkle with remaining sugar mixture. Dot with butter. Cover and chill 8 hours or overnight. Remove from refrigerator 30 minutes before baking. Bake, uncovered, at 350° for 1 hour or until a knife inserted near the center comes out clean. Let stand 5 minutes before serving. **Yield:** 4-6 servings.

ORANGE FRENCH TOAST

Larry Halblom, Sweet Home, Oregon

A few years ago, at the age of 50, I decided to teach myself to cook. I made this French toast that my mother would serve with grilled ham and sweet warm maple syrup. I was so pleased with the results, I've been cooking ever since!

    2 eggs, lightly beaten
    1 cup buttermilk
    4 teaspoons sugar
    1 teaspoon grated orange peel
1/4 teaspoon baking soda
1/4 teaspoon ground cinnamon
1/8 teaspoon salt
    6 slices day-old bread

In a bowl, combine eggs, buttermilk, sugar, orange peel, baking soda, cinnamon and salt. Soak bread for 2 minutes per side. Cook on a greased hot griddle until golden brown on both sides and cooked through. **Yield:** 2-4 servings.

PECAN-OATMEAL PANCAKES

Fred Schwierske, Mt. Horeb, Wisconsin

When I was a schoolteacher, these hearty pancakes—topped with my favorite syrup and fresh fruit—were the perfect energy booster for my hectic days. I still love their nutty flavor.

1-1/2 cups quick-cooking oats
    1 cup all-purpose flour
    2 tablespoons brown sugar
    2 teaspoons baking powder
1/4 teaspoon salt
1-1/2 cups milk
    2 eggs, lightly beaten
    2 tablespoons butter *or* margarine, melted
1/2 cup chopped pecans

In a bowl, combine oats, flour, brown sugar, baking powder and salt. Combine milk, eggs and butter; stir into dry ingredients just until blended. Fold in pecans. Pour batter by 1/4 cupfuls onto a lightly greased hot griddle; turn when bubbles form on top of pancakes. Cook until second side is golden brown. **Yield:** 14-16 pancakes.

BLUEBERRY FRENCH TOAST COBBLER

Marie Herr, Berea, Ohio

Each summer I pick fresh blueberries and freeze them with this family favorite in mind. It's a great way to recapture the warmth of past summer days on chilly winter Midwestern mornings.

4 eggs
1/2 cup milk
1 teaspoon vanilla extract
1/4 teaspoon baking powder
10 slices day-old French bread (3/4 inch thick)
4-1/2 cups unsweetened frozen blueberries
1/2 cup sugar
2 tablespoons butter *or* margarine, melted
1 teaspoon cornstarch
1 teaspoon ground cinnamon
1 tablespoon butter *or* margarine, softened

In a bowl, beat eggs, milk, vanilla and baking powder until smooth. Pour into a large shallow baking dish. Add bread slices, turning once to coat. Cover and chill for 8 hours or overnight. Combine blueberries, sugar, melted butter, cornstarch and cinnamon. Pour into a greased 13-in. x 9-in. x 2-in. baking dish. Cover and chill 8 hours or overnight. Remove both pans from refrigerator 30 minutes before baking. Place prepared bread on top of blueberry mixture. Spread softened butter on top. Bake, uncovered, at 400° for 30-35 minutes or until toast is golden brown and blueberries are bubbly. **Yield:** 6-8 servings.

HONEY NUT TOPPING

Susan Seymour, Valatie, New York

Because we often entertain for weekend brunches, I'm always looking for different recipes. This sweet and nutty topping for waffles or pancakes adds an elegant touch.

1/4 cup honey
1/4 cup sour cream
2 tablespoons chopped pecans

In a bowl, combine honey and sour cream until smooth. Add pecans; stir. Serve over waffles or pancakes. **Yield:** 2/3 cup.

BLUEBERRY SYRUP

Kate Stoehr, Dakota, Minnesota

When I was a girl, the only syrup my family ever used was maple. So when I was old enough, I was eager to make flavored syrups. This blueberry syrup gives a unique sweet flavor to pancakes and French toast.

12 pints fresh *or* frozen blueberries (about 6 pounds)
15 cups water, *divided*

10 cups sugar
1 package (1-3/4 ounces) powdered fruit pectin

Crush blueberries; place in a large kettle. Add 8 cups water. Bring to a full rolling boil; boil for 10 minutes, stirring constantly. Strain through a jelly bag, reserving juice. Empty contents from bag back into kettle; add 4 cups water. Bring to a full rolling boil; boil for 5 minutes. Pour back into jelly bag; strain. Combine juice; measure 10 cups of juice and place in the kettle. Add sugar, pectin and remaining water. Bring to a full rolling boil; boil for 5 minutes. Remove from the heat; let stand a few minutes. Skim off any foam. Pour hot into hot jars, leaving 1/4-in. headspace. Adjust caps. Process for 10 minutes in a boiling-water bath. **Yield:** 9 pints.

EGGNOG FRENCH TOAST

Robert Northrup, Las Cruces, New Mexico

This recipe is a favorite of our family not only at Christmas but anytime of the year. We especially like to prepare it when we go camping. It makes a hearty breakfast.

8 eggs
2 cups eggnog
1/4 cup sugar
1/2 teaspoon vanilla *or* rum extract
20 to 26 slices English muffin bread
Confectioners' sugar, optional
Maple syrup

In a bowl, beat eggs, eggnog, sugar and extract; soak bread for 2 minutes per side. Cook on a greased hot griddle until golden brown on both sides and cooked through. Dust with confectioners' sugar if desired. Serve with syrup. **Yield:** 8-10 servings.

POTATO WAFFLES

Annette Sheeley, Altona, Illinois

When I'm in a hurry and my family wants a hearty breakfast, I often make these easy waffles. You'll be pleasantly surprised by the subtle potato flavor.

1-1/3 cups instant potato flakes
1 cup all-purpose flour
2 teaspoons baking powder
1/2 teaspoon salt
2-1/4 cups milk
2 eggs, lightly beaten
1 tablespoon vegetable oil

In a mixing bowl, combine potato flakes, flour, baking powder and salt. Mix milk, eggs and oil; blend into dry ingredients. Bake in a preheated waffle iron according to manufacturer's directions until golden brown. **Yield:** 6-8 waffles (about 6-3/4 inches).

CHEDDAR FRENCH TOAST WITH DRIED FRUIT SYRUP

Jackie Lintz, Cocoa Beach, Florida
(PICTURED AT LEFT)

My family loves this warm French toast on cold mornings in the North Carolina mountains where we take our yearly vacation. Each year, I alter the recipe slightly by experimenting with different dried fruits.

    1-1/2 cups maple syrup
        1 package (8 ounces) dried fruit, diced
      1/4 cup chopped walnuts
       12 slices Italian *or* French bread (cut diagonally
            1 inch thick)
    1-1/3 cups shredded sharp cheddar cheese
        4 eggs
        2 cups milk
      1/4 teaspoon salt

Combine syrup, fruit and walnuts; let stand overnight. Cut a slit in the crust of each slice of bread to form a pocket. Stuff each pocket with 2 tablespoons cheese. In a bowl, beat eggs, milk and salt; soak bread for 2 minutes per side. Cook on a greased hot griddle until golden brown on both sides. Serve with dried fruit syrup. **Yield:** 6 servings.

PANCAKES WITH ORANGE HONEY BUTTER

LaDonna Reed, Ponca City, Oklahoma
(PICTURED AT LEFT)

Whenever I ask my family what they want for breakfast, they invariably ask for these pancakes. Not only are they light and fluffy, but my homemade orange honey butter adds a special sweet flavor.

    1-3/4 cups all-purpose flour
        1 teaspoon baking powder
        1 teaspoon baking soda
      1/2 teaspoon salt
    1-1/2 cups buttermilk
        3 eggs, lightly beaten
        2 tablespoons vegetable oil
        1 tablespoon honey
    ORANGE HONEY BUTTER:
      1/2 cup butter *or* margarine, softened
      1/3 cup honey
        2 tablespoons orange juice concentrate

In a mixing bowl, combine flour, baking powder, baking soda and salt. Combine buttermilk, eggs, oil and honey; add to dry ingredients and mix well. Pour batter by 1/4 cupfuls onto a lightly greased hot griddle; turn when bubbles form on top of pancakes. Cook until second side is golden brown. For or-

ange honey butter, combine butter and honey in a medium bowl; beat well. Stir in orange juice concentrate until smooth. Serve with pancakes. **Yield:** 12 pancakes.

BUTTERMILK WAFFLES

Darla Reynolds, Willmar, Minnesota
(PICTURED AT LEFT)

The recipe for these traditional waffles may seem plain, but the waffles are anything but! Everyone loves their extra-light texture and are delighted with their great taste.

        2 cups all-purpose flour
        2 teaspoons baking powder
        1 teaspoon baking soda
        1 teaspoon salt
        3 eggs, *separated*
        2 cups buttermilk
      2/3 cup sour cream
      1/2 cup vegetable oil
    Fresh apricot slices, optional
    Mint leaves, optional

In a mixing bowl, combine dry ingredients. In another bowl, beat egg yolks. Add buttermilk, sour cream and oil; stir into dry ingredients just until combined. Beat egg whites until stiff peaks form; fold into batter. Bake in a preheated waffle iron according to manufacturer's directions until golden brown. Garnish with apricots and mint leaves if desired. **Yield:** 14-16 waffles (4 inches).

FREEZER FRENCH TOAST

Diane Perry, Castro Valley, California

I don't care for prepackaged frozen French toast, but I rarely have time in the mornings to prepare it from scratch. Then my friend gave me this wonderful recipe. I keep a freezer full of these slices and simply pop them into the oven for a homemade breakfast in no time.

        4 eggs
        1 cup milk
        2 tablespoons sugar
        1 teaspoon vanilla extract
      1/4 teaspoon ground nutmeg
       10 slices day-old French bread (3/4 inch thick)
        1 to 2 tablespoons butter *or* margarine, melted

In a large bowl, beat eggs, milk, sugar, vanilla and nutmeg. Place bread in a well-greased 13-in. x 9-in. x 2-in. baking dish. Pour egg mixture over bread. Let soak for several minutes, turning bread once to coat. Freeze until firm. Package in airtight containers. To bake, place bread on a well-greased baking sheet. Dot with butter. Bake at 450° for 7 minutes; turn and bake 10-12 minutes longer or until golden brown. **Yield:** 4-5 servings.

> **DOWN-HOME GOODNESS.** *Pictured at left, clockwise from the bottom: Cheddar French Toast with Dried Fruit Syrup, Buttermilk Waffles and Pancakes with Orange Honey Butter (all recipes on this page).*

FRESH PEACH SAUCE
Dottye Wolf, Rolla, Missouri

I like to make my breakfast table as pretty as possible. This peach sauce adds a warm golden color to the table and terrific flavor to pancakes, waffles and French toast.

    1/2 cup water
      3 tablespoons sugar
      2 teaspoons cornstarch
Dash ground nutmeg
      1 cup sliced peeled fresh peaches
      1/8 to 1/4 teaspoon almond extract

In a saucepan, bring water, sugar, cornstarch and nutmeg to a boil; boil for 1 minute. Add peaches. Bring to a boil; boil another 1-2 minutes. Remove from the heat; stir in extract. Serve warm. **Yield:** 1-1/4 cups.

TRADITIONAL WAFFLES
Sharon Carbaugh, Central Valley, California

Once I made these light and tasty waffles for my family, they never let me use a prepackaged mix again! For that reason, I usually bake a double batch and freeze the leftovers. Then, on hurried mornings, I just pop them in the toaster for a quick meal.

2-1/4 cups all-purpose flour
      4 teaspoons baking powder
      2 eggs, lightly beaten
2-1/2 cups milk
      1/4 cup vegetable oil

In a bowl, combine flour and baking powder. Mix eggs, milk and oil; stir into dry ingredients just until combined. Bake in a preheated waffle iron according to manufacturer's directions until golden brown. **Yield:** 8-10 waffles (about 6-1/2 inches).

OVERNIGHT CARAMEL
FRENCH TOAST
Denise Goedeken, Platte Center, Nebraska

Because this recipe can be prepared the night before, it's perfect to serve overnight guests. So it gives you extra time to visit over morning coffee.

      1 cup packed brown sugar
      1/2 cup butter *or* margarine
      2 tablespoons light corn syrup
      12 slices white *or* whole wheat bread
      1/4 cup sugar
      1 teaspoon ground cinnamon, *divided*
      6 eggs
1-1/2 cups milk
      1 teaspoon vanilla extract

In a small saucepan over medium heat, bring brown sugar, butter and corn syrup to a boil, stirring constantly. Re-

move from the heat. Pour into a greased 13-in. x 9-in. x 2-in. baking dish. Top with six slices of bread. Combine sugar and 1/2 teaspoon cinnamon; sprinkle half over the bread. Place remaining bread on top. Sprinkle with remaining cinnamon-sugar; set aside. In a large bowl, beat eggs, milk, vanilla and remaining cinnamon. Pour over bread. Cover and chill 8 hours or overnight. Remove from refrigerator 30 minutes before baking. Bake, uncovered, at 350° for 30-35 minutes. **Yield:** 4-6 servings.

APPLE-CINNAMON SYRUP
Kathy Dance, Denfield, Ontario

Around our house, Saturday breakfasts are a time to relax. So I like to serve my family's favorite French toast topped with this homemade syrup. After such a satisfying meal, everyone slowly eases into their hectic day ahead.

      1/2 cup packed brown sugar
      1/3 cup water
      2 tablespoons butter *or* margarine
      1 teaspoon cornstarch
      1/2 teaspoon ground cinnamon
      3 medium apples, peeled and thinly sliced

In a saucepan over medium heat, bring brown sugar, water, butter, cornstarch and cinnamon to a boil; boil for 2 minutes until thick. Reduce heat to medium. Add apples; cook for 10-12 minutes or until apples are tender. **Yield:** about 2 cups.

STUFFED FRENCH TOAST
WITH BERRY SAUCE
Mary Kay Morris, Cokato, Minnesota

As the oldest of seven children growing up on a farm, if I wasn't milking the cows, I was making the meals. My love for cooking has continued through the years.

FILLING:
      1 package (8 ounces) cream cheese, softened
      1 tablespoon sugar
      1 teaspoon grated orange peel
      1/4 teaspoon ground cinnamon
FRENCH TOAST:
      2 eggs, lightly beaten
      1/4 cup milk
      1 teaspoon vanilla extract
      8 slices French bread (1 inch thick)
SYRUP:
      1/2 cup water
      1/4 cup maple syrup
      2 tablespoons sugar
      1 tablespoon cornstarch
1-1/2 cups loose-pack frozen blueberries

In a mixing bowl, beat cream cheese, sugar, orange peel and cinnamon until smooth; set aside. In a shallow bowl, combine eggs, milk and vanilla. Cut a pocket in the crust of each slice of bread. Stuff each pocket with 1-2 tablespoons filling. Dip bread in egg mixture on both sides. Fry on a greased hot griddle for 3-4 minutes per side or until golden brown. For syrup, combine water, maple syrup, sugar and cornstarch in a saucepan. Bring to a boil; boil 2 minutes to thicken. Reduce heat; add blueberries and simmer for 5-7 minutes or until berries are tender. Serve over French toast. **Yield:** 4-6 servings (1-1/2 cups syrup).

CORNFLAKE WAFFLES WITH HONEY SAUCE
Grace Gay, Franklin, Wisconsin

The great flavor of these waffles is enhanced by the crispness of the cornflakes and by the sweet honey sauce. I like to serve these with fresh fruit and sausages.

  1-1/4 cups all-purpose flour
    3/4 cup crushed cornflakes
      1 tablespoon baking powder
    1/4 teaspoon salt
      2 eggs, *separated*
  1-3/4 cups milk
    1/2 cup vegetable oil
HONEY SAUCE:
      1 cup honey
    1/2 cup maple syrup
    1/4 cup butter *or* margarine
    1/2 teaspoon ground cinnamon
Dash ground nutmeg

In a bowl, combine flour, cornflakes, baking powder and salt. Beat egg yolks lightly; add milk and oil. Stir into dry ingredients just until combined. Beat egg whites until stiff peaks form; fold into batter. Bake in a preheated waffle iron according to manufacturer's directions until golden brown. For honey sauce, combine honey, syrup, butter, cinnamon and nutmeg in a saucepan. Cook and stir on medium-low until heated through. **Yield:** 8-10 waffles (about 6-1/2 inches).

BANANA-STUFFED FRENCH TOAST
Susan Seymour, Valatie, New York

My family liked this French toast so much when they first tried it on vacation that I came up with my own version at home. Eating it brings back some wonderful memories.

      4 slices sourdough *or* Italian bread (1 inch thick)
      2 large ripe bananas
      2 eggs
    1/2 cup milk
      1 teaspoon vanilla extract
Maple syrup, optional

Cut a 3-in. pocket in the crust of each slice of bread. Slice the bananas in half lengthwise and then into 3-in. pieces. Place two pieces of banana in each pocket. In a shallow bowl, beat eggs, milk and vanilla; soak bread for 2 minutes on each side. Fry on a greased griddle over medium heat until golden brown on both sides. Serve with syrup if desired. **Yield:** 2-4 servings.

HOMEMADE PANCAKE MIX
Margareta Roduner, Cardinal, Ontario

I developed this convenient pancake mix to keep on hand for mornings when I'm pressed for time. Served with locally made maple syrup, these sweet and fluffy pancakes are a big hit.

PANCAKE MIX:
   10 cups all-purpose flour
   1/2 cup baking powder
     1 tablespoon salt
     2 cups shortening
PANCAKES:
 1-1/2 cups Pancake Mix
     1 tablespoon sugar
     1 cup milk
     1 egg, lightly beaten

In a large bowl, combine flour, baking powder and salt; mix well. Cut in shortening until mixture resembles coarse crumbs. Store in an airtight canister at room temperature. For pancakes, combine mix and sugar in a bowl. Combine milk and egg; add to dry ingredients and mix well. Pour batter by 1/3 cupfuls onto a lightly greased hot griddle; turn when bubbles form on top of pancakes. Cook until second side is golden brown. **Yield:** 6 pancakes.

GINGERBREAD WAFFLES
Ann Nace, Perkasie, Pennsylvania

Our family enjoys all types of waffles, but these are their favorite. They're softer than traditional waffles and the combination of spices provides a unique flavor. I hope your family enjoys them as much as mine does!

      1 cup all-purpose flour
  1-1/2 teaspoons baking powder
      1 teaspoon ground ginger
    3/4 teaspoon ground cinnamon
    1/2 teaspoon ground allspice
    1/2 teaspoon baking soda
    1/4 teaspoon dry mustard
    1/4 teaspoon salt
    1/3 cup packed brown sugar
      1 egg, *separated*
    3/4 cup buttermilk
    1/4 cup molasses
      3 tablespoons butter *or* margarine, melted
    1/3 cup chopped raisins
    1/8 teaspoon cream of tartar

In a bowl, combine flour, baking powder, ginger, cinnamon, allspice, baking soda, mustard and salt; set aside. In a large mixing bowl, beat brown sugar and egg yolk until fluffy. Add buttermilk, molasses and butter; stir into dry ingredients just until combined. Add raisins. In a small bowl, beat egg white and cream of tartar until soft peaks form. Gently fold into batter. Bake in a preheated waffle iron according to manufacturer's directions until golden brown. **Yield:** 6 waffles (about 4 inches).

BREADS & SPREADS

No breakfast is complete without oven-fresh breads and coffee cakes topped with scrumptious spreads. And don't forget sweet sticky doughnuts sure to satisfy everyone!

LEMON POPPY SEED BREAD

Karen Dougherty, Freeport, Illinois
(PICTURED AT LEFT)

The days that I have extra time for baking are few and far between. That's why this extra-quick bread is perfect. You and your family will love the ease of preparation and the delicious flavor.

    1 box (18-1/4 ounces) white cake mix without
      pudding
    1 package (3.4 ounces) instant lemon pudding mix
    4 eggs
    1 cup warm water
    1/2 cup vegetable oil
    4 teaspoons poppy seeds

In a mixing bowl, combine the cake and pudding mixes, eggs, water and oil; beat until well mixed. Fold in poppy seeds. Pour into two greased 9-in. x 5-in. x 3-in. loaf pans. Bake at 350° for 35-40 minutes or until bread tests done. Cool in pans for 10 minutes before removing to a wire rack. **Yield:** 2 loaves.

WHOLE WHEAT TOASTING BREAD

Evelyn Danby, Sarnia, Ontario
(PICTURED AT LEFT)

This recipe for whole wheat bread is one of my favorites. Try it topped with a fruit spread for a fast and flavorful breakfast.

    1 package (1/4 ounce) active dry yeast
    1/4 cup warm water (110° to 115°)
    1 cup warm milk (110° to 115°)
    1 tablespoon sugar
    2 tablespoons shortening
    1 egg
    1 teaspoon salt
    3-1/2 to 4 cups whole wheat flour
    1 tablespoon butter *or* margarine, melted

In a large mixing bowl, dissolve yeast in warm water. Add warm milk, sugar, shortening, egg, salt and 2 cups

---

of flour; beat until smooth. Add enough remaining flour to form a soft dough. Turn onto a floured board; knead until smooth and elastic, about 6-8 minutes. Place in a greased bowl, turning once to grease top. Cover and let rise in a warm place until doubled, about 1-1/2 hours. Punch dough down. Divide into thirds; roll each into a 12-in. rope. Braid ropes; place in a greased 8-1/2-in. x 4-1/2-in. x 2-1/2-in. loaf pan. Cover and let rise until doubled, about 45 minutes. Bake at 375° for 25-30 minutes. Remove from pan and brush with melted butter. Cool on a wire rack. **Yield:** 1 loaf.

WONDERFUL ENGLISH MUFFINS

Linda Rasmussen, Twin Falls, Idaho
(PICTURED AT LEFT)

When I was growing up on a farm, my mom always seemed to be making homemade bread...nothing tasted so good! Now I like to make these simple yet delicious muffins for my own family.

    1 cup milk
    1/4 cup butter *or* margarine
    2 tablespoons sugar
    1 teaspoon salt
    2 packages (1/4 ounce *each*) active dry yeast
    1 cup warm water (110° to 115°)
    2 cups all-purpose flour
    3 to 3-1/2 cups whole wheat flour
    1 tablespoon sesame seeds
    1 tablespoon poppy seeds
Cornmeal

Scald milk in a saucepan; add butter, sugar and salt. Stir until butter melts; cool to lukewarm. In a small bowl, dissolve yeast in warm water; add to milk mixture. Stir in all-purpose flour and 1 cup whole wheat flour until smooth. Add sesame seeds, poppy seeds and enough remaining whole wheat flour to make a soft dough. Turn onto a floured board; knead until smooth and elastic, about 8-10 minutes. Place in a greased bowl, turning once to grease top. Cover and let rise until doubled, about 1 hour. Punch dough down. Roll to 1/2-in. thickness on a cornmeal-covered surface. Cut into circles with a 3-1/2-in. or 4-in. cutter; cover with a towel and let rise until nearly doubled, about 30 minutes. Place muffins, cornmeal side down, in a greased skillet; cook over medium-low heat for 12-14 minutes or until bottoms are browned. Turn and cook about 12-14 minutes or until browned. Cool on wire racks; split and toast to serve. **Yield:** 12-16 muffins.

A SPREAD OF BREADS. *Pictured at left, clockwise from the bottom: Wonderful English Muffins, Lemon Curd, Whole Wheat Toasting Bread and Lemon Poppy Seed Bread (recipes on this page and page 50).*

LEMON CURD

Margaret Balakowski, Kingsville, Ontario
(PICTURED ON PAGE 48)

Besides canning and freezing our homegrown vegetables, I enjoy cooking and baking. I especially look forward to baking special treats for our granddaughter.

3 eggs
1 cup sugar
1/2 cup fresh lemon juice (about 2 lemons)
1/4 cup butter *or* margarine, melted
1 tablespoon grated lemon peel

In the top of a double boiler, beat eggs and sugar. Stir in lemon juice, butter and lemon peel. Cook over simmering water for 15 minutes or until thickened. **Yield:** 1-2/3 cups.

CARAMEL APPLE JAM

Robert Atwood, Wyoming, Michigan

I created this recipe one year when I had excess apples. The brown sugar gives the jam a wonderful caramel taste. I'm a retired master baker and cook who enjoys preparing Southern dishes for my wife of 48 years, two sons and five grandchildren.

6 cups diced peeled apples (1/8-inch cubes)
1/2 cup water
1/2 teaspoon butter *or* margarine
1 package (1-3/4 ounces) powdered fruit pectin
3 cups sugar
2 cups packed brown sugar
1/2 teaspoon ground cinnamon
1/4 teaspoon ground nutmeg

In a large kettle, mix apples, water and butter. Cook and stir over low heat until apples are soft. Stir in pectin; bring to a full rolling boil, stirring constantly. Stir in sugars, cinnamon and nutmeg. Return to a full rolling boil and boil for 1 minute, stirring constantly. Remove from the heat; skim off any foam. Pour hot jam into hot jars, leaving 1/4-in. headspace. Adjust caps. Process for 10 minutes in a boiling-water bath. **Yield:** 7 half-pints.

PENNSYLVANIA DUTCH POTATO DOUGHNUTS

Marlene Reichart, Leesport, Pennsylvania

My relatives have been making these tasty doughnuts for years. The potatoes keep them moist, and the glaze provides just the right amount of sweetness.

2-1/2 cups hot mashed *or* riced potatoes (no milk, butter or seasoning added)
1 cup milk
3 eggs, lightly beaten
2 tablespoons butter *or* margarine, melted
2 cups sugar
2 tablespoons baking powder
5 cups all-purpose flour

Cooking oil for deep-fat frying
GLAZE:
2 cups confectioners' sugar
5 tablespoons light cream
1/2 teaspoon vanilla extract

In a large bowl, combine potatoes, milk, eggs and butter. Combine sugar, baking powder and 2 cups flour; stir into potato mixture. Add enough remaining flour to form a soft dough. Divide dough in half. Turn onto a lightly floured board; roll each half to 1/2-in. thickness. Cut with a 2-3/4-in. doughnut cutter. In an electric skillet or deep-fat fryer, heat oil to 375°. Fry doughnuts, a few at a time, until golden, about 2 minutes. Turn with a slotted spoon and fry 2 more minutes or until golden. Drain on paper towels. Repeat until all doughnuts are fried. Combine glaze ingredients and drizzle over warm doughnuts. Serve immediately. **Yield:** about 4 dozen.

WHIPPED CREAM CHEESE

Rita Addicks, Weimar, Texas

When I want a break from butter or jams, I like to whip up this simple spread. All of the variations are wonderful and taste great on toasted breads.

1 package (8 ounces) cream cheese, softened
3 to 4 tablespoons milk

In a small mixing bowl, beat the cream cheese. Gradually beat in milk until light and fluffy. Serve on toast, English muffins or bagels. **Yield:** 1-1/2 cups. **Variations: Maple Cream Cheese**—Substitute maple syrup for milk. **Marmalade Cream Cheese**—Substitute 1/4 cup marmalade for milk. **Honey Cream Cheese**—Substitute 1/4 cup honey for milk.

PUMPKIN APPLE BUTTER

Robbin Runtas, Pewaukee, Wisconsin

A few years ago, I decided to try my hand at canning. This first recipe I tried was such a success that I've been canning like crazy ever since! You'll love the truly autumn flavor of this apple butter.

1 can (29 ounces) solid-pack pumpkin
2 cups apple cider
1 cup applesauce
1 cup packed light brown sugar
1 teaspoon ground cinnamon
1/2 teaspoon ground nutmeg
1/4 teaspoon ground cloves

In a large saucepan or Dutch oven, combine all ingredients. Simmer, uncovered, for 2 hours, stirring occasionally, until thickened. Pour into freezer containers. Refrigerate up to 1 month or freeze. **Yield:** 5 half-pints.

EASY LEMON-BLUEBERRY JAM

Joyce Robbins, Old Hickory, Tennessee

After one taste of this delightfully sweet and simple jam, people will find it hard to believe that you didn't spend many long hours in a hot kitchen. Of course, you don't have to let them in on your "secret"!

    4 cups fresh blueberries
    2 cups sugar
    1 package (3 ounces) lemon-flavored gelatin

In a large saucepan, slightly crush 2 cups of blueberries. Add remaining berries and sugar; mix well. Bring to a boil, stirring constantly. Remove from the heat; stir in gelatin until dissolved. Pour hot jam into jars or containers. Cover and cool. Refrigerate. **Yield:** 4 half-pints.

GRAHAM-STREUSEL COFFEE CAKE

Bonita Hellmich, Greensburg, Indiana

With three children and 500 acres to farm, my husband and I are busy to say the least! But we like to get our day off to a good start with a hearty breakfast that often includes this easy-to-prepare yet moist and delicious coffee cake.

STREUSEL:
    1-1/2 cups graham cracker crumbs
    1 cup packed brown sugar
    3/4 cup chopped pecans
    2/3 cup butter *or* margarine, melted
    2 teaspoons ground cinnamon
CAKE:
    1 box (18-1/4 ounces) white cake mix
        with pudding
    3 eggs, lightly beaten
    1 cup water
    1/4 cup vegetable oil

In a bowl, combine streusel ingredients; set aside. In a mixing bowl, combine cake mix, eggs, water and oil. Beat on low speed until mixed; beat on medium speed for 2 minutes. Pour half into a greased 13-in. x 9-in. x 2-in. baking pan. Sprinkle with half of the streusel. Carefully spread remaining batter over streusel. Top with remaining streusel. Bake at 350° for 35-40 minutes or until cake tests done. **Yield:** 12-16 servings.

RHUBARB RAISIN MARMALADE

Carmen Tuck, Airdrie, Alberta

At a retreat in the foothills of the Canadian Rockies, I sampled a marmalade combining rhubarb and raisins. I loved it so much that I went home and tried to duplicate it. I added the strawberries to make the marmalade even sweeter.

    2 medium oranges
    1 lemon
    6 cups sugar
    6 cups diced fresh *or* frozen rhubarb

1-1/2 cups chopped fresh *or* frozen strawberries
Pinch salt
    1 cup raisins

Finely grate orange and lemon peels; squeeze and reserve juices. In a large saucepan, combine peels, juices, sugar, rhubarb, strawberries and salt. Cook and stir over medium heat until sugar dissolves; add raisins. Bring to a full rolling boil; cook over medium heat until thick, about 5-10 minutes. Pour hot jam into hot jars, leaving 1/4-in. headspace. Adjust caps. Process for 10 minutes in a boiling-water bath. **Yield:** 4 pints.

CINNAMON APPLE BUTTER

Carol Johnson, Tipp City, Ohio

This is a recipe my 81-year-old mother has been making for years, and she's passed the recipe onto me. I enjoy making it for my five grandchildren—they love it on homemade bread.

    6 pounds apples, quartered
    2 cups apple cider
    5 cups sugar
    3 tablespoons cider vinegar
1-1/2 teaspoons ground cinnamon
    1 package (6 ounces) strawberry-flavored gelatin

In a large saucepan, cook apples in cider until tender. Press through a sieve or food mill; measure 10 cups apple pulp. Return to pan; add sugar, vinegar and cinnamon. Cook over medium heat for 20 minutes, stirring constantly. Stir in gelatin. Pour hot butter into hot jars, leaving 1/4-in. headspace. Adjust caps. Process for 10 minutes in a boiling-water bath. **Yield:** 6 pints.

CRANBERRY COFFEE CAKE

Imelda Nesteby, Decorah, Iowa

Even people who don't usually care for cranberries will love this warm and tasty coffee cake. And you'll be happy to know it's simple to make!

    2 cups all-purpose flour
    1 cup sugar
    2 teaspoons baking powder
    1/2 teaspoon salt
    1 cup milk
    2 tablespoons butter *or* margarine, melted
    2 cups fresh *or* frozen cranberries, halved
HOT BUTTER SAUCE:
    1/2 cup butter (no substitutes)
    1 cup sugar
    3/4 cup light cream
    1 teaspoon vanilla extract

In a bowl, combine flour, sugar, baking powder and salt. Combine milk and butter; add to dry ingredients and mix well. Fold in cranberries. Spread into a greased 9-in. square baking pan. Bake at 350° for 30-35 minutes or until cake tests done. For sauce, melt butter in a saucepan; gradually add sugar and cream. Simmer for 10 minutes. Remove from the heat; add vanilla. Serve over warm coffee cake. **Yield:** 9 servings.

BOUNTY OF BAKED GOODS. *Clockwise from lower left: Apricot Coffee Cake, Lemon Kolaches, Sticky Cinnamon Rolls, Snowflake Doughnuts and Danish Kringle (all recipes on pages 54 and 55).*

APRICOT COFFEE CAKE

Mary Alice Ramm, Muleshoe, Texas
(PICTURED ON PAGE 52)

My family just loves apricots, so whenever I get a chance, I try to make this coffee cake. Your family and friends will be impressed with its pretty appearance and great taste.

> 1 package (1/4 ounce) active dry yeast
> 1/4 cup warm water (110° to 115°)
> 3/4 cup warm milk (110° to 115°)
> 1 egg
> 1/2 cup butter *or* margarine, softened
> 4 to 4-1/2 cups all-purpose flour
> 1/2 cup sugar
> 1/2 teaspoon salt
> **APRICOT FILLING:**
> 12 ounces dried apricots
> 3/4 cup water
> 3/4 cup sugar
> 1/4 teaspoon ground cinnamon
> **GLAZE:**
> 1/2 cup confectioners' sugar
> 1 to 2 teaspoons milk
> 1/2 teaspoon butter *or* margarine, softened
> 1/2 teaspoon vanilla extract

In a large mixing bowl, dissolve yeast in warm water. Add warm milk, egg and butter; mix. Add 2-1/2 cups flour, sugar and salt; beat until smooth. Add enough remaining flour to form a soft dough. Turn onto a floured board; knead until smooth and elastic, about 6-8 minutes. Place in a greased bowl, turning once to grease top. Cover and let rise in a warm place until doubled, about 1 hour. For filling, combine apricots and water in a saucepan. Cover and simmer for 30 minutes. Cool 10 minutes. Pour into a blender; process at high speed until smooth. Stir in sugar and cinnamon; set aside. Punch dough down. Divide in half and roll each half into a 15-in. x 12-in. rectangle. Place on a greased baking sheet. Spread half of the filling in a 15-in. x 4-in. strip down center of dough. With a sharp knife, cut dough on each side of apricot filling into 1-in.-wide strips. Fold strips alternately across filling to give braided effect. Repeat with remaining dough and filling. Cover and let rise until doubled, about 30 minutes. Bake at 375° for 20 minutes or until golden brown. Cool on wire racks for 15 minutes. Combine glaze ingredients; drizzle over warm coffee cakes. Serve warm or allow to cool completely. **Yield:** 2 coffee cakes.

DANISH KRINGLE

Jeanne Hardaker, Quicksburg, Virginia
(PICTURED ON PAGE 53)

Everyone agrees that no store-bought kringle can top my homemade version. The nut filling and sweet glaze give this spectacular coffee cake great flavor.

> 2 cups all-purpose flour
> 1 tablespoon sugar
> 1/2 teaspoon salt
> 1/2 cup cold butter *or* margarine

> 1 package (1/4 ounce) active dry yeast
> 1/4 cup warm water (110° to 115°)
> 1/2 cup warm milk (110° to 115°)
> 1 egg, beaten
> **FILLING:**
> 1-1/2 cups finely chopped pecans *or* walnuts
> 1 cup packed brown sugar
> 1/2 cup butter *or* margarine, softened
> **GLAZE:**
> 1 cup confectioners' sugar
> 4 teaspoons water
> 1/2 teaspoon vanilla extract
> 2 tablespoons chopped pecans *or* walnuts

Combine flour, sugar and salt in a large bowl; cut in butter until mixture resembles fine crumbs. Dissolve yeast in warm water; stir into flour mixture with warm milk and egg. Beat until smooth (dough will be very soft). Cover and chill at least 2 hours but not more than 24 hours. Punch dough down. Divide dough in half; return one half to refrigerator. On a well-floured board, roll other half into a 15-in. x 6-in. rectangle. Combine filling ingredients. Spread half of the filling down center of rectangle in a 2-in. strip. Fold sides of dough over filling, overlapping 1-1/2 in.; pinch edges to seal. Shape into an oval; pinch ends together. Place seam side down on a greased 15-in. x 10-in. x 1-in. baking pan. Repeat with remaining dough and filling. Cover and let rise in a warm place for 30 minutes. Bake at 375° for 20-25 minutes or until golden brown. Cool for 15 minutes. Combine confectioners' sugar, water and vanilla; spread over the kringles. Sprinkle with nuts. **Yield:** 2 kringles.

LEMON KOLACHES

Eileen Weitnauer, Aitkin, Minnesota
(PICTURED ON PAGE 52)

I love to bake and try new recipes. These soft rolls are a favorite...I like to experiment by adding different flavors to the creamy filling.

> 2 packages (1/4 ounce *each*) active dry yeast
> 3/4 cup warm milk (110° to 115°)
> 1/2 cup sugar
> 1/2 cup butter *or* margarine, softened
> 1 teaspoon salt
> 3/4 teaspoon grated lemon peel
> 3 eggs
> 4-1/2 to 5 cups all-purpose flour
> **FILLING:**
> 1 package (8 ounces) cream cheese, softened
> 1/4 cup sugar
> 1 egg
> 1/2 teaspoon grated lemon peel

In a large mixing bowl, dissolve yeast in warm milk. Add sugar, butter, salt, lemon peel, eggs and 2 cups of flour; beat until smooth. Add enough remaining flour to form a soft dough. Turn onto a floured board; knead until smooth and elastic, about 6-8 minutes. Place in a greased bowl, turning once to grease top. Cover and let rise in a warm place until doubled, about 1 hour. Punch dough down. Divide in half; shape each half into 12 balls. Place 3 in. apart on greased baking sheets. Flatten each ball to a 3-in. circle. Cover and let rise in a warm place until doubled, about 30 minutes. In a small mixing bowl, beat all filling ingredients until smooth. Make a depression in the center of each roll; add filling. Bake at 375° for 8-10 minutes or until golden brown. Remove from pan to cool on a wire rack. **Yield:** 2 dozen.

SNOWFLAKE DOUGHNUTS

Alice Dunkin, Rock River, Wyoming
(PICTURED ON PAGE 53)

My family never cared for doughnuts much until they tried these. Their light-as-a-feather texture and golden color are so appealing.

2 packages (1/4 ounce *each*) active dry yeast
1 cup warm water (110° to 115°)
1-1/4 cups warm milk (110° to 115°)
1/2 cup vegetable oil
1/2 cup sugar
1/2 teaspoon salt
3 eggs
6 cups all-purpose flour
Cooking oil for deep-fat frying
Confectioners' sugar *or* additional sugar, optional

In a large mixing bowl, dissolve yeast in warm water. Add warm milk and oil. Add sugar, salt and eggs; mix well. Stir in flour (dough will be very sticky). Cover and let rise in a warm place until doubled, about 45 minutes. Stir down and let rise for 45 minutes. Stir down; roll out on a well-floured board to 1/2-in. thickness. Cut with a 2-1/2-in. cutter. Place on greased baking sheets; cover and let rise for 45 minutes. In an electric skillet or deep-fat fryer, heat 1 in. of oil to 350°. Fry the doughnuts, a few at a time, for 2 minutes per side or until browned. Drain on paper towels. Dust with sugar if desired. **Yield:** about 3 dozen. **Editor's Note:** This is a very soft dough, but makes wonderfully light doughnuts.

DELICIOUS DOUGHNUTS. Allow freshly made doughnuts to stand for 15-20 minutes before deep-frying. They'll be firm and delectable!

STICKY CINNAMON ROLLS

Carrie Williams, Elkhart, Kansas
(PICTURED ON PAGE 52)

What would breakfast be without cinnamon rolls? My family likes them served fresh from the oven either with or without the sweet frosting. I hope your family likes them, too!

2 packages (1/4 ounce *each*) active dry yeast
3/4 cup sugar, *divided*
1/2 cup warm water (110° to 115°)

2 cups warm milk (110° to 115°)
3/4 cup shortening
1-1/2 teaspoons salt
2 eggs
7-3/4 to 8-1/4 cups all-purpose flour
2 tablespoons butter *or* margarine, melted
TOPPING:
1 cup sugar
1/4 cup packed brown sugar
2 tablespoons ground cinnamon
ICING (optional):
1 cup confectioners' sugar
2 to 3 tablespoons milk
1 teaspoon vanilla extract

In a large mixing bowl, dissolve yeast and 1/4 cup sugar in warm water. Add warm milk, shortening, salt, eggs and 3 cups flour; beat until smooth. Add enough remaining flour to form a soft dough. Turn onto a floured surface; knead until smooth and elastic, about 6-8 minutes. Place in a greased bowl, turning once to grease top. Cover and let rise in a warm place until doubled, about 1 hour. Punch dough down. Divide into thirds. Roll each portion into a 12-in. x 8-in. rectangle; spread with butter. Combine topping ingredients and sprinkle over butter. Roll up tightly, starting at long end. Slice into 1-in. rolls. Place in three greased 11-in. x 7-in. x 2-in. baking pans. Let rise until nearly doubled, about 30 minutes. Bake at 350° for 20-30 minutes or until lightly browned. Remove from pans to wire racks to cool. If desired, make icing: Beat all ingredients until smooth and ice cooled rolls. **Yield:** 3 dozen.

BLUEBERRY BREAKFAST CAKE

Colette Jaworski, Buford, Georgia

I like to prepare this coffee cake on weekends...especially during blueberry season. Served with fresh fruit, it's a nice switch from eggs, cereal and pancakes.

2 cups all-purpose flour
1/2 cup sugar
2 teaspoons baking powder
1 egg, lightly beaten
1/2 cup milk
1/4 cup butter *or* margarine, softened
1 teaspoon grated lemon peel
2 cups fresh *or* frozen blueberries
TOPPING:
1/3 cup sugar
1/4 cup all-purpose flour
1/4 cup finely chopped walnuts
1/2 teaspoon ground cinnamon
3 tablespoons cold butter *or* margarine

In a mixing bowl, combine flour, sugar and baking powder. Add egg, milk, butter and lemon peel; mix just until dry ingredients are moistened. Fold in the blueberries. Spread in a greased 9-in. square baking pan. For topping, combine sugar, flour, walnuts and cinnamon. Cut in butter until mixture is crumbly. Sprinkle over batter. Bake at 350° for 40-45 minutes or until cake tests done. **Yield:** 9 servings.

COCOA CINNAMON SPREAD

Dorothy Woodson, El Cajon, California

If you like cinnamon toast—and who doesn't—you'll want to keep plenty of this quick and easy spread on hand. It's especially nice to give as gifts for the holidays.

    1 pound (2 cups) butter *or* margarine, softened
    1 box (1 pound) confectioners' sugar
    2 to 3 tablespoons baking cocoa
    2 to 3 tablespoons ground cinnamon

In a mixing bowl, beat butter, sugar, cocoa and cinnamon until smooth. Spread on hot toast. **Yield:** 4 cups.

BLUSHING PEACH JAM

Cheryl Hall, Osceola, Indiana
(PICTURED AT RIGHT)

My husband, son and I live on 10 acres where we tend a large garden and acres of pumpkins. We love this jam so much we're going to start growing raspberries, too.

    2 cups crushed peeled peaches
    2 cups red raspberries, crushed
    1/4 cup lemon juice
    7 cups sugar
    2 pouches (3 ounces *each*) liquid fruit pectin
    1/8 teaspoon almond extract

In a large kettle, combine peaches, raspberries and lemon juice. Stir in sugar; mix well. Bring to a full rolling boil, stirring constantly. Boil for 1 minute. Remove from the heat. Stir in pectin; return to a full rolling boil. Boil 1 minute, stirring constantly. Remove from the heat; cool for 5 minutes. Skim off foam. Add extract. Pour hot jam into hot jars, leaving 1/4-in. headspace. Adjust caps. Process for 15 minutes in a boiling-water bath. **Yield:** 4 pints.

APPLE PIE JAM

Audrey Godell, Stanton, Michigan
(PICTURED AT RIGHT)

Although I've been canning for years, I've never found a good apple jam recipe, so I created this one. My husband of 41 years and I love this jam so much because it tastes just like apple pie...without the crust!

    4 to 5 large Golden Delicious apples, peeled and
       sliced (about 2 pounds)
    1 cup water
    5 cups sugar
    1/2 teaspoon butter *or* margarine
    1 pouch (3 ounces) liquid fruit pectin
 1-1/2 teaspoons ground cinnamon
    1 teaspoon ground nutmeg
    1/4 teaspoon ground mace, optional

In a large kettle, combine apples and water. Cover and cook slowly just until tender. Measure 4-1/2 cups apples; return to the kettle. (Discard the rest or save for another recipe.) Add sugar and butter to kettle; bring to a full rolling

boil, stirring constantly. Stir in pectin; return to a full rolling boil. Boil 1 minute, stirring constantly. Remove from the heat; stir in spices. Skim off foam. Pour hot jam into hot jars, leaving 1/4-in. headspace. Adjust caps. Process for 10 minutes in a boiling-water bath. **Yield:** 7 half-pints.

ENGLISH MUFFIN BREAD

Elsie Trippett, Jackson, Michigan
(PICTURED AT RIGHT)

Most of my cooking and baking is from scratch, and I think it's worth the time and effort. Everyone enjoys homemade goodies like this delicious bread.

    5 cups all-purpose flour, *divided*
    2 packages (1/4 ounce *each*) active dry yeast
    1 tablespoon sugar
    2 teaspoons salt
    1/4 teaspoon baking soda
    2 cups warm milk (120° to 130°)
    1/2 cup warm water (120° to 130°)
Cornmeal

In a large mixing bowl, combine 2 cups flour, yeast, sugar, salt and baking soda. Add warm milk and water; beat on low speed for 30 seconds, scraping bowl occasionally. Beat on high for 3 minutes. Stir in remaining flour (batter will be stiff). Do not knead. Grease two 8-1/2-in. x 4-1/2-in. x 2-1/2-in. loaf pans. Sprinkle pans with cornmeal. Spoon batter into the pans and sprinkle cornmeal on top. Cover and let rise in a warm place until doubled, about 45 minutes. Bake at 375° for 35 minutes or until golden brown. Remove from pans immediately to cool on wire racks. **Yield:** 2 loaves.

CINNAMON PLUM JAM

Eloise Neeley, Norton, Ohio
(PICTURED AT RIGHT)

When I share this slightly sweet jam with family and friends, it disappears quickly. Through the years, I've learned to make more than one batch!

    7 cups sugar
    5 cups coarsely ground peeled plums (about
       2-1/2 pounds)
    1/2 cup water
    1/3 cup lemon juice
    1 package (1-3/4 ounces) powdered fruit pectin
    1/2 teaspoon ground cinnamon

In a large kettle, combine sugar, plums, water and lemon juice. Bring to a full rolling boil, stirring constantly. Stir in pectin; return to a full rolling boil. Boil 1 minute, stirring constantly. Remove from the heat; stir in cinnamon. Skim off foam. Pour hot jam into hot jars, leaving 1/4-in. headspace. Adjust caps. Process for 10 minutes in a boiling-water bath. **Yield:** 7 half-pints.

> **SPREADING IT ON THICK.** *Pictured at right, clockwise from the bottom: Blushing Peach Jam (in jar and on bread), Apple Pie Jam, Cinnamon Plum Jam and English Muffin Bread (all recipes on this page).*

CINNAMON PLUM JAM

STRAWBERRY-RHUBARB JAM

Hazel Keller, Peshtigo, Wisconsin

Like lots of people, I find myself with an abundance of rhubarb each summer. One year I found this recipe and I've been making it ever since. The sweetness of the strawberries really complements the tart rhubarb.

- **3 cups fresh *or* frozen strawberries**
- **6 cups sugar, *divided***
- **3 cups diced fresh *or* frozen rhubarb**
- **1 teaspoon grated lemon *or* lime peel**

In a large saucepan, crush strawberries. Stir in 4 cups of sugar. Add rhubarb and lemon peel. Bring to a full rolling boil over medium-high heat; boil 4 minutes. Add remaining sugar; return to a full rolling boil. Boil 4 minutes more. Remove from the heat; skim off any foam. Pour hot jam into hot jars, leaving 1/4-in. headspace. Adjust caps. Process for 10 minutes in a boiling-water bath. **Yield:** 3 pints.

LUSCIOUS LEMON COFFEE CAKE

Lois McAtee, Oceanside, California

The holidays are a time for special meals, but it's also a season of too little time! That's why this is my favorite coffee cake...year-round. It's so simple to prepare, but it's very flavorful.

TOPPING:
- **1 cup chopped walnuts**
- **1/2 cup sugar**
- **2 teaspoons ground cinnamon**

CAKE:
- **1 package (18-1/4 ounces) yellow cake mix without pudding**
- **1 package (3.4 ounces) instant lemon pudding mix**
- **1 cup (8 ounces) sour cream**
- **4 eggs, lightly beaten**
- **1/2 cup vegetable oil**

Combine topping ingredients and set aside. In a mixing bowl, combine cake and pudding mixes, sour cream, eggs and oil. Mix on medium speed for 2 minutes. Pour half into a greased 13-in. x 9-in. x 2-in. baking pan. Sprinkle half of the topping over batter. Spoon remaining batter over topping and spread evenly. Sprinkle with remaining topping. Bake at 350° for 30-35 minutes or until cake tests done. **Yield:** 12-16 servings.

PEAR CAKE WITH SOUR CREAM TOPPING

Norma Bluma, Emporia, Kansas

This is a great way to combine bread and fruit for an all-in-one breakfast. The cake is very tasty and the unique topping is simply delicious.

- **1/2 cup butter *or* margarine, softened**
- **1/2 cup sugar**
- **3 eggs, lightly beaten**

- **1 teaspoon grated lemon peel**
- **1-3/4 cups all-purpose flour**
- **2 teaspoons baking powder**
- **1 teaspoon salt**
- **1/2 cup milk**
- **1 can (29 ounces) pear halves, drained**

TOPPING:
- **1 cup (8 ounces) sour cream**
- **2 tablespoons brown sugar**
- **1 tablespoon grated lemon peel**

In a mixing bowl, cream butter and sugar. Add eggs and lemon peel; mix well. Combine flour, baking powder and salt; add to creamed mixture alternately with milk. Beat well. Spread batter into a greased 13-in. x 9-in. x 2-in. baking pan. Slice pear halves and arrange in rows on top of batter. Mix topping ingredients until smooth; spread over pears. Bake at 350° for 30-35 minutes or until cake tests done. **Yield:** 12-16 servings.

PULL-APART MORNING ROLLS

Bernadine Stine, Roanoke, Indiana

Family members often come to our farm for down-home country breakfasts. These easy-to-prepare cinnamon rolls are always part of the menu.

- **1 cup chopped walnuts**
- **1 package (3.4 ounces) instant butterscotch pudding mix**
- **1/2 cup packed brown sugar**
- **1/2 teaspoon ground cinnamon**
- **2 packages (13-1/2 to 15 ounces *each*) frozen dinner roll dough, thawed**
- **1/2 cup butter *or* margarine, melted**

Sprinkle walnuts in the bottom of a well-greased 10-in. fluted tube pan. Combine pudding mix, brown sugar and cinnamon. Roll each dinner roll in butter and then in brown sugar mixture; coat well. Place each roll in pan. Cover and refrigerate overnight. Remove from refrigerator 30 minutes before baking. Bake at 375° for 30-35 minutes or until golden brown. Cool 10 minutes in pan before removing to a serving platter. **Yield:** 16-20 servings.

ORANGE COFFEE CAKE

Marie Fairchild, Paxton, Illinois

My husband and I enjoy country living on our 120-acre farm where we grow corn and soybeans. I often prepare this refreshingly different coffee cake for breakfast or a midday snack.

- **1/4 cup butter *or* margarine, softened**
- **3/4 cup sugar**

2 eggs
1 tablespoon orange juice
1 tablespoon grated orange peel
1-1/2 cups all-purpose flour
2 teaspoons baking powder
1/4 teaspoon salt
1/2 cup milk
TOPPING:
1/2 cup sugar
1/2 teaspoon ground cinnamon
2 tablespoons butter *or* margarine, melted

In a mixing bowl, cream butter and sugar. Beat in eggs, one at a time. Add orange juice and peel. Combine flour, baking powder and salt; add to creamed mixture alternately with milk. Pour into a greased 9-in. square baking pan. For topping, combine sugar and cinnamon; sprinkle over batter. Drizzle with butter. Bake at 375° for 30 minutes or until cake tests done. **Yield:** 9 servings.

HEART-SHAPED COFFEE CAKE

Jane Pierce, Schertz, Texas

My family likes me to put all of my "heart" into making breakfast, and this special coffee cake is one they request often. The recipe feeds a crowd, but you'll be delighted (and surprised!) by how quickly your family will gobble it up.

2 packages (1/4 ounce *each*) active dry yeast
1/2 cup warm water (110° to 115°)
2 cups (16 ounces) sour cream
1/3 cup sugar
1/4 cup butter *or* margarine, softened
2 eggs, lightly beaten
2 teaspoons salt
5-1/2 to 6 cups all-purpose flour
1 can (21 ounces) cherry pie filling
1 egg white, beaten
1 tablespoon butter *or* margarine, melted
GLAZE:
1-1/2 cups confectioners' sugar
3 to 4 teaspoons milk
1 teaspoon vanilla extract

In a large bowl, dissolve yeast in warm water; add sour cream, sugar, butter, eggs, salt and 2 cups flour. Beat until smooth. Add enough remaining flour to form a soft dough. Turn onto a floured board; knead until smooth and elastic, about 6-8 minutes. Place in a greased bowl, turning once to grease top. Cover and let rise in a warm place until doubled, about 1 hour. Punch dough down; divide in half. On a lightly floured surface, roll each half into a 20-in. x 10-in. rectangle. Place each on a greased baking sheet. On both long sides of each rectangle, make 2-in. cuts at 1/2-in. intervals. Spread pie filling down the center of each rectangle; crisscross strips over filling. Shape and stretch coffee cakes to form right and left halves of heart. Cover and let rise until doubled, about 50 minutes. Brush dough gently with egg white. Bake at 375° for 25-30 minutes or until lightly browned. While warm, brush with butter. Cool on wire racks. Combine glaze ingredients. When coffee cakes have cooled, place heart halves together; drizzle glaze over heart. **Yield:** 18-20 servings.

HEARTY SAUSAGE LOAF

Ann Maibach, Sterling, Ohio

Finding fun and different breakfast recipes is a real challenge, so was I happy when I stumbled upon this one! You're family and friends will love the meal-in-one appeal of this breakfast loaf.

2 loaves (1 pound *each*) frozen bread dough, thawed
1 pound bulk pork sausage
1 garlic clove, minced
1/8 teaspoon fennel seed
3 eggs, lightly beaten
2 cups (8 ounces) shredded mozzarella cheese
1/4 cup grated Romano *or* Parmesan cheese
1 tablespoon butter *or* margarine, melted

Allow dough to rise until nearly doubled. Meanwhile, brown sausage with garlic and fennel seed in a skillet. Drain and cool. Add eggs and cheeses; mix well. Punch dough down and roll each loaf into a 16-in. x 12-in. rectangle. Place half of the sausage mixture on each rectangle, spreading to within 1 in. of edges. Roll jelly-roll style, starting at a narrow end. Place on a greased baking sheet. Bake at 375° for 30-35 minutes. Brush with melted butter while warm. Cut into 1-in. slices. **Yield:** 16-20 servings.

HONEY GRANOLA BREAD

Connie Kleinwort, Fargo, North Dakota

I've made this bread for several occasions, and it always gets rave reviews. The granola gives it a wonderful texture that makes it perfect for toast in the morning and also for sandwiches.

5 to 5-1/2 cups all-purpose flour, *divided*
1 cup granola cereal
2 packages (1/4 ounce *each*) active dry yeast
2 teaspoons salt
1-1/2 cups water
1 cup plain yogurt
1/2 cup honey
1/4 cup vegetable oil
2 eggs
2 cups whole wheat flour

In a large mixing bowl, combine 3 cups all-purpose flour, granola, yeast and salt; blend well. In a medium saucepan, combine water, yogurt, honey and oil; heat to 120°-130°. Add to flour mixture along with eggs; mix on low until moistened. Beat for 3 minutes at medium speed. Stir in whole wheat flour and 1 cup all-purpose flour to form a soft dough. Turn onto a floured board; knead about 8-10 minutes, adding enough remaining all-purpose flour until dough is smooth and elastic. Place in a greased bowl, turning once to grease top. Cover and let rise in a warm place until doubled, about 1 hour. Punch dough down. Shape into two loaves; place in greased 9-in. x 5-in. x 3-in. loaf pans. Cover and let rise until doubled, about 45 minutes. Bake at 350° for 35-40 minutes. Remove from pans to cool on wire racks. **Yield:** 2 loaves.

CREAM CHEESE BREAD

Janet Kowalski, Brookfield, Wisconsin

You're sure to impress family and friends with the attractive appearance and great-tasting flavor of this bread. It takes some time to prepare, but it's worth it!

BREAD:
- 2 packages (1/4 ounce *each*) active dry yeast
- 1/2 cup warm water (110° to 115°)
- 1 cup (8 ounces) sour cream
- 1/2 cup butter *or* margarine, melted
- 1/2 cup sugar
- 2 eggs, lightly beaten
- 1/2 teaspoon salt
- 4 cups all-purpose flour

FILLING:
- 2 packages (8 ounces *each*) cream cheese, softened
- 1 egg, lightly beaten
- 3/4 cup sugar
- 2 teaspoons vanilla extract
- 1/2 teaspoon salt

GLAZE:
- 2 cups confectioners' sugar
- 2 teaspoons vanilla extract
- 3 to 4 tablespoons milk

In a large bowl, dissolve yeast in warm water. Stir in sour cream, butter, sugar, eggs and salt. Add flour; stir until smooth. Cover and refrigerate overnight. The next morning, combine all filling ingredients and set aside. Meanwhile, punch dough down and divide into six equal portions. Turn one portion onto a floured board and roll into a 12-in. x 8-in. rectangle. Spread with a sixth of the filling. Roll up from one of the long sides; seal seams and fold ends under. Place on a greased baking sheet. Repeat with remaining dough and filling. Using scissors, cut 3/4 in. deep into sides of each roll at 3/4-in. intervals, alternating from one side to the other. Cover and let rise in a warm place until almost doubled, about 45 minutes. Bake at 375° for 18-20 minutes or until golden brown. Cool 10 minutes before removing to wire racks. For glaze, combine sugar and vanilla. Gradually add milk until glaze is of spreading consistency; drizzle over warm bread. **Yield:** 6 loaves.

CHOCOLATE CINNAMON BUNS

Pat Habiger, Spearville, Kansas

Chocolate lovers will rejoice when you put out a platter of these fresh-from-the-oven rolls dripping with icing. Eat them by themselves for a real sweet treat or serve them as a finale to your breakfast feast.

- 1 package (1/4 ounce) active dry yeast
- 3/4 cup warm water (110° to 115°)
- 2-1/4 cups all-purpose flour
- 1/2 cup plus 3 tablespoons sugar, *divided*
- 1/3 cup baking cocoa
- 1/4 cup shortening
- 1 teaspoon salt
- 1 egg

- 1 tablespoon butter *or* margarine, softened
- 1-1/2 teaspoons ground cinnamon

ICING:
- 3/4 cup confectioners' sugar
- 1 to 2 tablespoons milk

Dissolve yeast in warm water; set aside. In a mixing bowl, combine flour, 1/2 cup sugar, cocoa, shortening, salt and egg. Add yeast mixture to form a soft dough. Knead five to 10 times. Place in a greased bowl, turning once to grease top. Cover and let rise until doubled, about 1 hour. Punch down. Turn onto a floured board and roll out to a 15-in. x 9-in. rectangle. Spread butter over dough. Mix cinnamon and remaining sugar; sprinkle over butter. Roll up jelly-roll style. Slice into 1 in. rolls. Place in a greased 11-in. x 7-in. x 2-in. baking pan. Cover and let rise until doubled, about 45 minutes. Bake at 375° for 20-25 minutes. Combine icing ingredients; drizzle over warm rolls. Serve immediately. **Yield:** 15 rolls.

CHEERY CHERRY BREAD

Carol Van Sickle, Versailles, Kentucky

These loaves are especially pretty at Christmastime, when I make enough to share with friends and neighbors. Everyone raves about the flavor.

- 3 eggs, lightly beaten
- 2-1/2 cups all-purpose flour
- 2 cups grated carrots
- 1-1/2 cups flaked coconut
- 1 cup sugar
- 1/2 cup milk
- 1/2 cup vegetable oil
- 1 teaspoon baking powder
- 1 teaspoon baking soda
- 1/2 cup maraschino cherries

In a mixing bowl, combine the first nine ingredients; mix well. Fold in cherries. Spoon into three greased 7-1/2-in. x 3-3/4-in. x 2-1/4-in. loaf pans. Bake at 350° for 40-45 minutes or until bread tests done. **Yield:** 3 loaves.

ENHANCE THE FLAVOR *of quick breads by storing them overnight before slicing and serving.*

OVERNIGHT BERRY COFFEE CAKE

Susan Drenth, South Holland, Illinois

After enjoying a berry coffee cake at a bed-and-breakfast we visited on our honeymoon, I went home and tried to duplicate it. My husband said I was successful!

- 2 cups all-purpose flour
- 1 cup sugar
- 1/2 cup packed brown sugar
- 1 teaspoon baking powder
- 1 teaspoon baking soda
- 1 teaspoon ground cinnamon

   1/2 teaspoon salt
     1 cup buttermilk
   2/3 cup butter *or* margarine, melted
     2 eggs, beaten
     1 cup fresh *or* frozen raspberries *or* blueberries
TOPPING:
   1/2 cup packed brown sugar
   1/2 cup chopped nuts
     1 teaspoon ground cinnamon

In a large bowl, combine flour, sugars, baking powder, baking soda, cinnamon and salt. In a separate bowl, combine buttermilk, butter and eggs; add to dry ingredients and mix until well blended. Fold in berries. Pour into a greased 13-in. x 9-in. x 2-in. baking pan. Combine topping ingredients; sprinkle over batter. Cover and refrigerate several hours or overnight. Uncover and bake at 350° for 45-50 minutes or until cake tests done. **Yield:** 12-16 servings.

BANANA FRITTERS

Laurel Cosbie, Palm Desert, California

Soon after I made these fritters for the first time, my husband began requesting them on a regular basis. I also like to serve them to overnight guests as a sweet breakfast treat.

     2 eggs
   1/2 cup milk
     1 teaspoon vegetable oil
     1 cup all-purpose flour
     1 teaspoon baking powder
     1 teaspoon salt
     4 large firm bananas
Cooking oil for deep-fat frying
Confectioners' sugar, optional

In a bowl, beat eggs, milk and oil. Combine flour, baking powder and salt; stir into egg mixture until smooth. Cut bananas into quarters (about 2 in. long). Dip each banana piece into batter to coat. In an electric skillet or deep-fat fryer, heat oil to 375°. Fry banana pieces, two to three at a time, until golden brown. Drain on paper towels. Dust with confectioners' sugar if desired. **Yield:** 6-8 servings.

NUTTY LEMON COFFEE CAKE

Cecilia Knox, Deerfield Beach, Florida

One morning about 20 years ago, a neighbor invited me over to help her "taste" this new recipe. Now every time I make this delicious coffee cake, it reminds me of my good friend back in Ohio.

     1 cup butter *or* margarine, softened
     1 cup sugar
     3 eggs
     1 cup (8 ounces) sour cream
     1 teaspoon vanilla extract
     1 teaspoon lemon extract
  2-1/2 cups all-purpose flour
  2-1/2 teaspoons baking powder
     1 teaspoon baking soda

   1/8 teaspoon salt
TOPPING:
     1 cup ground pecans
   1/2 cup sugar
     1 teaspoon ground cinnamon

In a mixing bowl, cream butter and sugar. Add eggs, one at a time, beating well after each addition. In another bowl, mix sour cream and extracts. Combine flour, baking powder, baking soda and salt; add to creamed mixture alternately with sour cream mixture. Mix well. Spread half in a greased 13-in. x 9-in. x 2-in. baking pan. Combine topping ingredients; sprinkle half over batter. Carefully spread remaining batter on top; sprinkle with remaining topping. Bake at 350° for 30-35 minutes or until cake tests done. **Yield:** 16-20 servings.

STRAWBERRY BREAD

Shirley Durham, Poplar Bluff, Missouri

My husband and I are strawberry lovers, so each spring we pick about 30 quarts. This recipe makes two delicious loaves. One we eat right away; the other we freeze and pull out when family comes to visit.

     3 cups all-purpose flour
     2 cups sugar
     1 teaspoon ground cinnamon
     1 teaspoon salt
     1 egg plus 3 egg whites, lightly beaten
  1-1/4 cups vegetable oil
     2 cups chopped fresh *or* frozen strawberries
  1-1/2 cups chopped walnuts

In a large bowl, combine flour, sugar, cinnamon and salt. Add egg, egg whites and oil; stir just until moistened. Fold in strawberries and nuts. Spoon into two greased 8-1/2-in. x 4-1/2-in. x 2-1/2-in. loaf pans. Bake at 350° for 70 minutes or until bread tests done. Cool in pans 10 minutes before removing to a wire rack. **Yield:** 2 loaves.

CHERRY-RASPBERRY JAM

Lenora McCulley, Reedsville, Wisconsin

When sour cherries and red raspberries are in season, I always freeze some with this recipe in mind. I've been making jams and jellies for years, and friends and family agree this is the best I make.

  2-1/2 cups finely chopped *or* ground sour cherries
     (about 1-1/2 pounds)
     2 cups red raspberries
     5 cups sugar
     1 package (1-3/4 ounces) powdered fruit pectin

In a large kettle, combine cherries and raspberries; stir in sugar. Bring to a full rolling boil, stirring constantly. Add pectin; return to a full rolling boil. Boil 1 minute, stirring constantly. Remove from the heat; skim off foam. Pour hot jam into hot jars, leaving 1/4-in. headspace. Adjust caps. Process for 10 minutes in a boiling-water bath. **Yield:** 6 half-pints.

SWISS BUTTERHORNS

Cheryl Paulsen, Granville, Iowa
(PICTURED AT LEFT)

My husband and I like to entertain at breakfast, and we're always looking for new recipes. So I was thrilled when my daughter shared this butterhorn recipe with me. They're so rich, light and easy to make.

DOUGH:
    2 cups all-purpose flour
    1/4 teaspoon salt
    1/2 cup cold margarine
    1/3 cup cold butter
    1 egg yolk, lightly beaten
    3/4 cup sour cream
FILLING:
    1/2 cup chopped pecans
    1/2 cup sugar
    1 teaspoon ground cinnamon
GLAZE (optional):
    1 cup confectioners' sugar
    2 tablespoons milk
    1/4 teaspoon vanilla extract

In a large bowl, combine flour and salt. Cut in margarine and butter until crumbly. Stir in egg yolk and sour cream; shape into a ball. Chill several hours or overnight. Divide dough into thirds. On a well-floured board, roll each portion into a 12-in. circle. Combine filling ingredients. Sprinkle a third of the filling over each circle. Cut each circle into 12 wedges. Roll each wedge, starting at the wide end. Place on greased baking sheets with points down. Bake at 350° for 15-18 minutes or until lightly browned. Make glaze if desired: Combine all ingredients and spread on warm rolls. **Yield:** 3 dozen.

HOLIDAY SOUR CREAM RINGS

Lois McAtee, Oceanside, California
(PICTURED AT LEFT)

These delicious sour cream rings have become part of our traditional Christmas breakfast. But my family and friends love the sweet flavor so much, I find myself making them throughout the year as well.

    2 packages (1/4 ounce *each*) active dry yeast
    1/4 cup warm water (110° to 115°)
    2 eggs, lightly beaten
    2 cups (16 ounces) sour cream
    2/3 cup sugar
    1/3 cup butter *or* margarine, melted
    1-1/2 teaspoons salt
    1 teaspoon ground mace
    1 teaspoon ground cardamom

GIFTS FROM THE KITCHEN. *Pictured at left, clockwise from the top: Holiday Sour Cream Rings, Cranberry Orange Loaf and Swiss Butterhorns (all recipes on this page).*

    5-3/4 to 6-1/2 cups all-purpose flour
    1/2 cup *each* raisins, chopped candied pineapple
      and chopped candied cherries
    1 tablespoon brandy *or* orange juice
    1-1/3 cups confectioners' sugar
    4 to 6 teaspoons orange juice
Whole candied cherries

In a large mixing bowl, dissolve yeast in warm water. Add eggs, sour cream, sugar, butter, salt, mace, cardamom and 3 cups flour; beat until smooth. Add enough remaining flour to form a soft dough. Turn onto a floured board; knead until smooth and elastic, about 6-8 minutes. Place in a greased bowl, turning once to grease top. Cover and let rise in a warm place until doubled, about 1 hour. Meanwhile, combine raisins, pineapple, cherries and brandy or orange juice; mix well and set aside. Punch dough down. Pat into a 16-in. x 12-in. rectangle. Sprinkle with fruit. Fold over and knead lightly to distribute fruit. Divide dough into sixths. Roll each portion into a 16-in. rope. Place two ropes on a greased baking sheet. Intertwine them seven to eight times, joining ends to form a ring. Repeat with remaining dough. Cover and let rise until nearly doubled, about 45 minutes. Bake at 350° for 30-35 minutes or until golden. Cool 15 minutes. Combine confectioners' sugar and orange juice; spread over rings. Decorate with candied cherries. **Yield:** 3 loaves.

CRANBERRY ORANGE LOAF

Peggy Frazier, Indianapolis, Indiana
(PICTURED AT LEFT)

I'm a true morning person who loves entertaining at breakfast. It's so much fun to get up early, set a pretty table and share a delicious breakfast with friends.

    2 cups all-purpose flour
    1 cup sugar
    1-1/2 teaspoons baking powder
    1 teaspoon baking soda
    1/2 teaspoon salt
    1 egg
    1/2 cup orange juice
Grated peel of 1 orange
    2 tablespoons butter *or* margarine, melted
    2 tablespoons hot water
    1 cup fresh *or* frozen cranberries
    1 cup chopped walnuts

Combine flour, sugar, baking powder, baking soda and salt in a large mixing bowl. In a small bowl, beat egg; add orange juice, peel, butter and water. Stir into dry ingredients just until moistened. Fold in cranberries and nuts. Spoon into a greased 9-in. x 5-in. x 3-in. loaf pan or two 5-in. x 2-1/2-in. x 2-in. mini-loaf pans. Bake at 325° for 1 hour or until bread tests done. Cool in pan for 10 minutes before removing to a wire rack. **Yield:** 1 loaf or 2 mini-loaves.

PUMPKIN BREAD

Shirley Sober, Granada Hills, California

A friend of mine graciously shared her "secret recipe" for this bread with me. It's become such a family favorite that I'm not allowed to enter my family's get-togethers without this bread in hand!

    1 cup butter *or* margarine, softened
    3 cups sugar
    3 eggs
    3 cups all-purpose flour
    1 tablespoon baking powder
1-1/2 teaspoons baking soda
1-1/2 teaspoons ground cinnamon
1-1/2 teaspoons ground cloves
1-1/2 teaspoons ground nutmeg
    1 can (16 ounces) solid-pack pumpkin

In a mixing bowl, cream butter and sugar. Add eggs; mix well. Combine dry ingredients; stir into creamed mixture just until moistened. Stir in pumpkin. Pour into two greased 9-in. x 5-in. x 3-in. loaf pans. Bake at 350° for 1 hour or until bread tests done. **Yield:** 2 loaves.

SOUTHERN GAL BISCUITS

Kay Curtis, Guthrie, Oklahoma

When I got married, I made sure to copy this recipe of my mom's. I'm glad I did...it's become one of my husband's favorites. We especially like to eat them smothered with homemade country sausage gravy.

    2 cups all-purpose flour
    2 tablespoons sugar
    4 teaspoons baking powder
1/2 teaspoon salt
1/2 teaspoon cream of tartar
1/2 cup shortening
    1 egg
2/3 cup milk

In a bowl, combine flour, sugar, baking powder, salt and cream of tartar. Cut in shortening until mixture resembles fine crumbs. In a small bowl, beat egg and milk; stir into dry ingredients just until moistened. Turn onto a lightly floured surface; roll to 1/2-in. thickness. Cut with a 2-1/2-in. biscuit cutter. Bake at 400° for 12-15 minutes or until golden brown. **Yield:** about 1 dozen.

PRUNE-FILLED DANISH

Margaret Pache, Mesa, Arizona

When I'm short on time, I often find myself making this simple yet tasty danish. You'll love the quick and easy crust and the subtle prune flavor.

    1 package (12 ounces) pitted prunes, halved
    1 cup water

    2 tubes (8 ounces *each*) refrigerated
      crescent rolls
    1 can (15 ounces) coconut-pecan frosting, *divided*
    2 tablespoons butter *or* margarine, melted,
      divided
1/2 cup confectioners' sugar

In a saucepan, bring prunes and water to a boil. Cover; remove from the heat and let stand 10 minutes. Drain, reserving juice. Unroll one tube of rolls and pat into the bottom of a greased 13-in. x 9-in. x 2-in. baking pan. Spread with half of the frosting. Cover with prunes. Mix 1 tablespoon butter and 1 tablespoon reserved prune juice; drizzle over prunes. Roll out remaining rolls into a 13-in. x 9-in. rectangle. Place over prunes. Combine remaining frosting and butter with 1 tablespoon prune juice. Carefully spread over dough. Bake at 375° for 25-30 minutes or until golden brown. Cool for 10 minutes. Mix confectioners' sugar with 1 to 2 tablespoons prune juice; drizzle over cake. (Discard remaining prune juice.) **Yield:** 12-16 servings.

BREAKFAST NUT ROLL

Josephine Buss, Neenah, Wisconsin

This is one of my favorite recipes that I have been making for years—I even won a prize for it years ago. It's special not only because it tastes so good, but because it was passed down to me by my dear aunt.

    2 cups all-purpose flour
1/2 teaspoon salt
3/4 cup cold butter *or* margarine
    1 package (1/4 ounce) active dry yeast
1/2 cup plus 1 teaspoon sugar
1/4 cup warm water (110° to 115°)
    2 eggs, *separated*
    1 teaspoon vanilla extract
1/2 cup chopped walnuts
Confectioners' sugar

In a large bowl, combine flour and salt; cut in butter until crumbly; set aside. In a small bowl, dissolve yeast and 1 teaspoon sugar in warm water; let stand 10 minutes. Beat egg yolks; add to yeast mixture. Stir gently into flour mixture to form a smooth ball. Divide dough in half; turn onto a floured board. Roll each half into a 12-in. x 8-in. rectangle. Beat egg whites until stiff peaks form; beat in remaining sugar. Fold in vanilla. Spread onto each rectangle; sprinkle with nuts. Starting with short edge, roll up jelly-roll style. Pinch ends together. Place on a greased baking sheet. Cut a deep slit down center of each roll (do not cut through). Immediately bake at 375° for 25-30 minutes or until golden brown. Dust with confectioners' sugar while warm. When cooled completely, slice diagonally. **Yield:** 2 rolls.

SPICED RHUBARB BREAD
Thelma Terpstra, Lynden, Washington

We have so much rhubarb in the Northwest, I was happy to get another idea for its uses. I especially like this recipe because it freezes well.

1-1/2 cups packed brown sugar
2/3 cup vegetable oil
1 egg
1 cup buttermilk
1 teaspoon vanilla extract
1 teaspoon baking soda
2-1/2 cups all-purpose flour
1 teaspoon salt
1 teaspoon ground cinnamon
1-1/2 cups diced fresh *or* frozen rhubarb
1/2 cup chopped nuts, optional
TOPPING:
1/2 cup sugar
1 tablespoon butter *or* margarine, melted
1 teaspoon ground cinnamon

In a mixing bowl, beat brown sugar, oil and egg. Add buttermilk, vanilla and baking soda; mix well. Combine flour, salt and cinnamon; stir into milk mixture. Fold in rhubarb and nuts if desired. Pour into two greased 8-1/2-in. x 4-1/2-in. x 2-1/2-in. loaf pans. Combine topping ingredients; sprinkle over loaves. Bake at 350° for 1 hour or until bread tests done. **Yield:** 2 loaves.

BLUEBERRY BRUNCH LOAF
Jean Nietert, Claremont, South Dakota

I like to make special breakfasts on the weekend for my husband and children. This recipe's sweet frosting really makes the already delicious blueberry bread even more tasty.

1/4 cup butter *or* margarine, softened
3/4 cup packed brown sugar
1 egg
1 tablespoon grated orange peel
2-1/4 cups all-purpose flour
1 tablespoon baking powder
1/2 teaspoon salt
1/2 cup milk
1/4 cup orange juice
1 cup fresh *or* frozen blueberries
GLAZE:
1/2 cup confectioners' sugar
2 teaspoons butter *or* margarine, softened
1/2 teaspoon grated orange peel
1 to 1-1/2 tablespoons milk

In a mixing bowl, cream butter and brown sugar. Stir in egg and orange peel. Combine flour, baking powder and salt; add to creamed mixture alternately with milk and juice, mixing thoroughly after each addition. Fold in blueberries. Pour into a greased 9-in. x 5-in. x 3-in. loaf pan. Bake at 350° for 50-55 minutes or until bread tests done. Cool in pan 10 minutes before removing to a wire rack. For

glaze, combine sugar, butter and orange peel. Gradually add milk until glaze is of spreading consistency; drizzle over warm bread. Cool completely. **Yield:** 1 loaf.

ZUCCHINI SNACK BREAD
Julie Engan, Post Falls, Idaho

Dad drove a logging truck through the beautiful forests and farmlands of northern Idaho's panhandle. Some days I would join him, and Mom would send along this moist bread for us to snack on.

3 cups all-purpose flour
2-1/4 teaspoons ground cinnamon
1-1/4 teaspoons salt
1 teaspoon baking soda
1/4 teaspoon baking powder
1/4 teaspoon ground nutmeg
3 eggs
2 cups sugar
1 cup vegetable oil
1 tablespoon vanilla extract
2 cups shredded zucchini
1 cup chopped walnuts

Combine flour, cinnamon, salt, baking soda, baking powder and nutmeg; set aside. In a mixing bowl, lightly beat eggs; stir in sugar, oil and vanilla. Add dry ingredients; stir just until moistened. Fold in zucchini and nuts; mix well (batter will be stiff). Pour into two greased and floured 8-1/2-in. x 4-1/2-in. x 2-1/2-in. loaf pans. Bake at 350° for 50-60 minutes or until bread tests done. Cool in pans 10 minutes before removing to a wire rack. **Yield:** 2 loaves.

THANKSGIVING BREAD
Kathryn Detweiler, West Farmington, Ohio

This bread combines two Thanksgiving standbys—cranberries and pumpkin. Serve it on the big day or make it with leftovers from your Thanksgiving feast.

2 eggs
2 cups sugar
1 cup cooked *or* canned pumpkin
1/2 cup vegetable oil
2-1/4 cups all-purpose flour
1 tablespoon pumpkin pie spice
1 teaspoon baking soda
1/2 teaspoon salt
1 cup chopped fresh *or* frozen cranberries

In a mixing bowl, beat eggs and sugar. Add pumpkin and oil; mix well. Add dry ingredients; stir just until moistened. Fold in cranberries. Spoon into two greased 8-1/2-in. x 4-1/2-in. x 2-1/2-in. loaf pans. Bake at 350° for 50-55 minutes or until bread tests done. Cool in pans 10 minutes before removing to wire racks. **Yield:** 2 loaves.

RASPBERRY COFFEE CAKE

Lisa Schulz, Madison, Wisconsin
(PICTURED AT LEFT)

This fresh and fruity coffee cake looks elegant but is so simple to make. I like to serve it to guests for special breakfasts and brunches. Because someone always asks me for the recipe, I usually write it out ahead of time!

   1 loaf (1 pound) frozen bread *or* sweet bread
      dough, thawed
   1 pint fresh raspberries
 1/2 cup all-purpose flour
 1/4 cup sugar
 1/4 cup cold butter *or* margarine
 1/8 teaspoon vanilla extract
GLAZE:
 1/2 cup confectioners' sugar
   3 to 4 teaspoons milk

Roll dough into a greased 13-1/4-in. pizza pan. Bake at 350° for 5 minutes. Sprinkle with berries. Combine flour and sugar; cut in butter and vanilla until crumbly. Sprinkle over berries. Bake at 350° for 25-30 minutes or until golden. Cool. Combine glaze ingredients; drizzle over coffee cake. **Yield:** 8-10 servings.

CIDER DOUGHNUTS

Suzanne Christensen, Defiance, Iowa
(PICTURED AT LEFT)

Here on our 1,250-acre farm, we usually have a quick breakfast on the go. So I often keep a batch of these light and moist doughnuts on hand. They disappear quickly because no one can eat just one!

 2/3 cup packed brown sugar
   2 eggs
   1 teaspoon ground nutmeg
 3/4 teaspoon salt
 1/4 teaspoon ground cinnamon
 1/4 teaspoon ground allspice
 1/4 teaspoon ground cardamom
   6 tablespoons butter *or* margarine, melted
      and cooled
   1 cup apple cider
   3 cups all-purpose flour
 1/2 cup whole wheat flour
   2 teaspoons baking powder
 1/2 teaspoon baking soda
Cooking oil for deep-fat frying
Confectioners' sugar, optional

In a mixing bowl, beat the first seven ingredients until thick, about 5 minutes. Gradually beat in butter, then cider. Combine flours, baking powder and baking soda. Add to batter; beat just until blended. Cover and refrigerate 1 hour. Divide

> **TASTY TREATS.** *Pictured at left, clockwise from the bottom: Raspberry Coffee Cake, Cider Doughnuts and English Scones (all recipes on this page).*

dough in half. Turn onto a lightly floured surface; pat to 1/2-in. thickness. Cut with a floured 2-1/2-in. doughnut cutter. Repeat with remaining dough. In an electric skillet or deep-fat fryer, heat oil to 375°. Fry doughnuts, a few at a time, for 2 minutes per side. Drain on paper towels. Dust with confectioners' sugar if desired. **Yield:** about 1-1/2 dozen.

ENGLISH SCONES

Barry Grieve, Fort Campbell, Kentucky
(PICTURED AT LEFT)

When I came to America from England in 1967, I made sure to bring along my favorite recipe for scones. Served warm with butter, they're perfect for breakfast.

   2 cups all-purpose flour
 1/2 cup sugar
   2 teaspoons baking powder
 1/4 cup cold butter *or* margarine
   1 cup raisins
 1/2 cup milk
   1 egg
Additional milk

In a bowl, combine flour, sugar and baking powder. Cut in butter until mixture resembles fine crumbs. Stir in raisins. Beat milk and egg; add to dry ingredients, stirring lightly. Turn onto a lightly floured board; roll to 1-in. thickness. Cut with a 2-1/2-in. biscuit cutter. Place on an ungreased baking sheet. Brush with milk. Bake at 425° for 10-15 minutes or until golden brown. **Yield:** 10 scones.

BUTTERMILK COFFEE CAKE

Fran Pugh, Stockton, California

Of all the things I make for breakfast, this gets eaten the fastest. That's all right with me because it's also the easiest to prepare! Serve this tasty treat with fresh fruit, juice and coffee for a complete meal.

2-1/2 cups all-purpose flour
   1 cup packed brown sugar
 3/4 cup sugar
 3/4 cup vegetable oil
   1 teaspoon salt
   1 egg, lightly beaten
   1 cup buttermilk
   1 teaspoon baking soda
TOPPING:
   1 cup chopped pecans
 1/4 cup packed brown sugar
 1/4 cup sugar
   1 tablespoon all-purpose flour
 3/4 teaspoon ground cinnamon
 1/2 teaspoon ground nutmeg

In a mixing bowl, combine flour, sugars, oil and salt; mix well. Remove 1/2 cup and set aside. To remaining flour mixture, add egg, buttermilk and baking soda; mix well. Pour into a greased 15-in. x 10-in. x 1-in. baking pan. To reserved flour mixture, add all topping ingredients; mix well. Sprinkle over batter. Bake at 350° for 25-30 minutes or until cake tests done. **Yield:** 20-24 servings.

BREAKFAST COOKIES

Wanda Cox, Roscommon, Michigan

I like to give my family a hearty start in the morning, especially when they have to eat in a hurry. These easy-to-make "cookies" are perfect for breakfast on the run and really appeal to the kid in all of us.

- 2/3 cup butter *or* margarine, softened
- 2/3 cup sugar
- 1 egg, lightly beaten
- 1 teaspoon vanilla extract
- 3/4 cup all-purpose flour
- 1/2 teaspoon baking soda
- 1/2 teaspoon salt
- 1-1/2 cups old-fashioned oats
- 1/2 cup wheat germ
- 1 cup (4 ounces) shredded cheddar cheese
- 6 bacon strips, cooked and crumbled

In a mixing bowl, cream butter and sugar. Add egg and vanilla; mix well. Combine flour, baking soda and salt; add to creamed mixture and mix well. Stir in oats and wheat germ. Fold in cheese and bacon. Drop by rounded teaspoonsful onto ungreased baking sheets. Bake at 350° for 15-17 minutes or until light brown. **Yield:** about 3 dozen.

APRICOT-NUT SPREAD

Ruth Stenson, Santa Ana, California

This nice and tart spread can add extra-special flavor to homemade muffins and biscuits, especially when the baked goodies are fresh from the oven.

- 1 package (6 ounces) dried apricots
- 1/2 cup water
- 1 package (8 ounces) cream cheese, cubed and softened
- 1/2 cup chopped walnuts

Soak apricots in water overnight; drain; reserving 2 tablespoons liquid. Place apricots and reserved liquid in a blender or food processor. Process for about 10 seconds. Add cream cheese; process just until blended, about 10-20 seconds. Add walnuts and blend until mixed. Store in the refrigerator. **Yield:** 2 cups.

SUNSHINE BISCUITS

Kim Norman, Chandler, Arizona

These golden biscuits really bring sunshine to my breakfast table, especially on cold winter mornings when they're served with butter and molasses.

- 2 cups all-purpose flour
- 1 cup cornmeal
- 2 tablespoons sugar
- 4-1/2 teaspoons baking powder
- 3/4 teaspoon cream of tartar
- 1/2 teaspoon salt

- 3/4 cup cold butter *or* margarine
- 1 egg, lightly beaten
- 1 cup milk

In a bowl, combine flour, cornmeal, sugar, baking powder, cream of tartar and salt. Cut in butter until mixture resembles coarse crumbs. Combine egg and milk; stir into flour mixture just until moistened. Let stand 5 minutes. Turn onto a floured board; knead for about 1 minute. Pat or roll out to 3/4-in. thickness; cut with a 3-in. biscuit cutter. Place on a greased baking sheet. Bake at 450° for 10-12 minutes. **Yield:** about 1 dozen.

SWEET POTATO BREAD

Joan Helms, Quitaque, Texas

We raise and sell sweet potatoes on our farm in the lower part of the Texas panhandle. Years ago, a customer shared his wife's sweet potato bread recipe with me. It's been a family favorite ever since.

- 3 cups sugar
- 3 eggs, lightly beaten
- 2 cups cold mashed sweet potatoes
- 1 teaspoon vanilla extract
- 3 cups all-purpose flour
- 1 teaspoon baking powder
- 1 teaspoon ground nutmeg
- 1 teaspoon ground allspice
- 1 teaspoon ground cinnamon
- 1/2 teaspoon salt
- 1/2 teaspoon baking soda
- 1 cup chopped pecans, optional

In a mixing bowl, combine sugar, eggs, sweet potatoes and vanilla; mix well. Combine flour, baking powder, nutmeg, allspice, cinnamon, salt and baking soda; stir into potato mixture. Fold in nuts if desired. Pour into two greased 8-1/2-in. x 4-1/2-in. x 2-1/2-in. loaf pans. Bake at 350° for 1 hour or until bread tests done. Cool in pans 10 minutes before removing to a wire rack to cool completely. **Yield:** 2 loaves.

BANANA NUT BREAD

Susan Jones, La Grange Park, Illinois

This quick bread is a family favorite, so I always seem to have ripe bananas on hand especially for this recipe. I'm sure your family will love this tasty nutty bread as much as mine.

- 1/4 cup butter *or* margarine, softened
- 3/4 cup sugar
- 2 eggs
- 3/4 cup mashed ripe bananas (about 2 medium)
- 1/2 cup sour cream
- 2-1/4 cups all-purpose flour
- 1 teaspoon ground cinnamon
- 3/4 teaspoon baking soda
- 1/2 teaspoon salt
- 1/2 cup chopped walnuts

In a mixing bowl, cream the butter, sugar and eggs, mixing

well. Stir in bananas and sour cream. Stir in dry ingredients just until moistened. Fold in nuts. Pour into a greased 8-1/2-in. x 4-1/2-in. x 2-1/2-in. loaf pan. Bake at 350° for 1 hour or until bread tests done. Cool in pan 10 minutes before removing to a wire rack. **Yield:** 1 loaf.

BLUEBERRY QUICK BREAD

Jill Williams, Charlottesville, Indiana

Most prepackaged quick bread mixes contain very little fruit. But this recipe calls for lots of juicy berries, so it's guaranteed to be moist and delicious.

    5 cups all-purpose flour
1-1/2 cups sugar
    2 tablespoons baking powder
    1 teaspoon salt
    3/4 cup cold butter *or* margarine
1-1/2 cups chopped walnuts
    4 eggs
    2 cups milk
    2 teaspoons vanilla extract
    3 cups fresh *or* frozen blueberries

In a large bowl, combine flour, sugar, baking powder and salt. Cut in butter until mixture resembles coarse crumbs. Stir in walnuts. In a small bowl, beat eggs, milk and vanilla; stir into dry ingredients just until moistened. Gently fold in blueberries. Pour into two 9-in. x 5-in. x 3-in. loaf pans. Bake at 350° for 20 minutes or until bread tests done. Cool in pan 10 minutes before removing to a wire rack. **Yield:** 2 loaves.

 **FAST AND FLAVORFUL.** *Make raspberry butter in a hurry. Just combine 1 cup softened butter, 2 cups confectioners' sugar and 1 package (10 ounces) frozen raspberries (thawed). Mix until smooth.*

CORN SCONES

Lorna Lamont, Dominion City, Manitoba

My family really enjoys these hearty scones—they're a nice change from usual muffins and biscuits. They're also nice to have on hand for when unexpected company drops in...which seems to be often!

3-1/2 cups all-purpose flour
    2 tablespoons baking powder
    1 teaspoon dry mustard
1/2 teaspoon salt
    3/4 cup cold butter *or* margarine
1-1/2 cups (6 ounces) shredded cheddar cheese
    1 can (15 ounces) cream-style corn
    2 eggs, lightly beaten
    2 tablespoons milk

In a medium bowl, combine flour, baking powder, mustard and salt. Cut in butter until the mixture resembles coarse crumbs. Stir in cheese, corn and eggs until a soft dough forms. Turn onto a floured board, kneading gently 10-12 times or until dough is no longer sticky. Roll out to 1-in. thickness; cut with a 2-1/2-in. or 3-in. cutter. Place on an ungreased baking sheet. Brush with milk. Bake at 425° for 20-25 minutes or until golden brown. Serve warm. **Yield:** 10-15 scones.

CRUNCHY APPLE BREAD

Myrtle Young, Astoria, Oregon

Here on our farm where we raise shorthorn cattle, I enjoy baking for my husband of over 40 years, our children and grandkids. And at the holidays, I make plenty of loaves of apple bread to share with friends.

2/3 cup shortening
1/2 cup sugar
1/2 cup packed brown sugar
    2 eggs
1/4 cup orange juice
    2 cups all-purpose flour
1/2 teaspoon baking soda
1/4 teaspoon salt
    1 cup diced peeled apple
    3/4 cup raisins
    3/4 cup chopped pecans

In a mixing bowl, cream shortening and sugars. Add eggs and orange juice; beat well. Combine flour, baking soda and salt; stir into creamed mixture. Stir in apple, raisins and pecans. Pour into a greased 9-in. x 5-in. x 3-in. loaf pan. Bake at 350° for 55-60 minutes or until bread tests done. Cool in pan 10 minutes before removing to a wire rack. **Yield:** 1 loaf.

EASY GERMAN BISCUITS

Elma Dreiling, Wichita, Kansas

My mother-in-law, who was of German descent, gave me this delicious recipe for easy yeast biscuits. It's so special because it goes back in her family for generations.

    1 package (1/4 ounce) active dry yeast
1/2 cup warm water (110° to 115°)
2-1/2 cups all-purpose flour
    1/3 cup sugar
    2 teaspoons baking powder
    1 teaspoon salt
1/4 teaspoon baking soda
    1 cup buttermilk
1/4 cup vegetable oil

Dissolve yeast in warm water. In a large bowl, combine flour, sugar, baking powder, salt and baking soda. Add yeast mixture, buttermilk and oil; stir well. Cover and refrigerate at least 12 hours. Punch down. Turn onto a floured board and roll out to 1-in. thickness. Cut with a 2-in. biscuit cutter and place 2 in. apart on a greased baking sheet. Bake at 400° for 12 minutes. **Yield:** 15 biscuits. **Editor's Note:** Dough will keep in refrigerator for 2 weeks.

Cookin' Up...
MAGNIFICENT MUFFINS

These marvelous homemade muffins are guaranteed to please your entire family, whether they like their muffins sweet and light or packed with hearty ingredients.

BREAKFAST IN A MUFFIN

Janne Rowe, Wichita, Kansas
(PICTURED AT LEFT)

For a change of pace from sweet muffins, I like to make these. They're loaded with lots of flavor and perfect for mornings when you need to eat on the run.

    1 cup whole wheat flour
    1 cup all-purpose flour
1/4 cup sugar
    4 teaspoons baking powder
1/4 teaspoon salt
    1 cup milk
1/4 cup vegetable oil
    2 eggs, *divided*
    1 package (8 ounces) cream cheese, softened
1/4 cup shredded cheddar cheese
1/4 teaspoon seasoned salt
    4 bacon strips, cooked and crumbled

In a large bowl, combine first five ingredients. Combine milk, oil and 1 egg; stir into dry ingredients just until moistened. Fill greased or paper-lined muffin cups half full. In a mixing bowl, beat cream cheese and second egg. Add cheddar cheese and seasoned salt; mix well. Stir in bacon. Spoon 2 tablespoons in the center of each muffin. Bake at 425° for 15-20 minutes or until muffins test done. Serve warm. **Yield:** about 1 dozen.

PUMPKIN-APPLE MUFFINS WITH STREUSEL TOPPING

Carolyn Riley, Carlisle, Pennsylvania
(PICTURED AT LEFT)

Mother always made these tasty muffins whenever the family gathered at her house. Now they're a favorite of not only my own family, but of my in-laws' as well.

2-1/2 cups all-purpose flour
    2 cups sugar
    1 tablespoon pumpkin pie spice
    1 teaspoon baking soda

MOUTH-WATERING MORSELS. *Pictured at left, clockwise from bottom: Breakfast in a Muffin, Pumpkin-Apple Muffins with Streusel Topping and Maple-Drizzled Apple Muffins (all recipes on this page).*

1/2 teaspoon salt
    2 eggs, lightly beaten
    1 cup canned pumpkin
1/2 cup vegetable oil
    2 cups finely chopped peeled apples
TOPPING:
1/4 cup sugar
    2 tablespoons all-purpose flour
1/2 teaspoon ground cinnamon
    1 tablespoon butter *or* margarine

In a large bowl, combine flour, sugar, pumpkin pie spice, baking soda and salt. Combine eggs, pumpkin and oil; stir into dry ingredients just until moistened. Fold in apples. Fill greased or paper-lined muffin cups three-fourths full. For topping, combine sugar, flour and cinnamon. Cut in butter until mixture resembles coarse crumbs; sprinkle 1 teaspoon over each muffin. Bake at 350° for 30-35 minutes or until muffins test done. Cool in pan 10 minutes before removing to a wire rack. **Yield:** about 1-1/2 dozen.

MAPLE-DRIZZLED APPLE MUFFINS

Sarah Brodersen, Herman, Nebraska
(PICTURED AT LEFT)

I've been baking for years and enjoy seeing the smiles on family members' faces whenever they sample one of my treats...like these delicious muffins!

1-1/3 cups all-purpose flour
    1 cup quick-cooking oats
  2/3 cup sugar
    1 tablespoon baking powder
1-1/2 teaspoons ground cinnamon
  1/2 cup milk
  1/3 cup butter *or* margarine, melted
  1/4 cup maple syrup
    1 egg, lightly beaten
    2 cups chopped peeled apples
   12 pecan halves
GLAZE:
  1/3 cup confectioners' sugar
    2 tablespoons maple syrup

In a large bowl, combine flour, oats, sugar, baking powder and cinnamon. In small bowl, mix milk, butter, syrup and egg; stir into dry ingredients just until moistened. Fold in apples. Fill greased or paper-lined muffin cups three-fourths full. Top each with a pecan half. Bake at 400° for 18-20 minutes or until muffins test done. Cool in pan 10 minutes before removing to wire rack. Cool completely. For glaze, mix sugar and syrup; drizzle over muffins. **Yield:** about 1 dozen.

RIVER'S BEND BLUEBERRY MUFFINS

Joan Theriault, Caribou, Maine

As the owner of a bed-and-breakfast, I'm always looking for new great-tasting breakfast recipes. So when I discovered this blueberry muffin recipe, it immediately became a "standard" with the country breakfast I serve my guests.

        2 cups all-purpose flour
  1-1/4 cups sugar
        2 teaspoons baking powder
        1 to 2 teaspoons ground nutmeg
  Dash salt
        2 eggs, lightly beaten
    1/2 cup butter *or* margarine, melted
    1/2 cup buttermilk
    1/2 teaspoon vanilla extract
        2 cups fresh blueberries

In a bowl, combine flour, sugar, baking powder, nutmeg and salt. Combine eggs, butter, buttermilk and vanilla; stir into dry ingredients just until moistened. Gently fold in blueberries. Fill greased or paper-lined muffin cups two-thirds full. Bake at 375° for 20-25 minutes or until muffins test done. Cool in pan 10 minutes before removing to a wire rack. **Yield:** about 1 dozen.

SPOON MUFFINS

Treva Latta, Valley Center, Kansas

This standard muffin recipe has to be one of my all-time favorites. I like to make them as is or with blueberries added to the batter. No matter how they're prepared, everyone agrees that the best way to eat them is hot from the oven slathered with sweet creamy butter!

        1 package (1/4 ounce) active dry yeast
        2 cups warm water (110° to 115°)
        4 cups self-rising flour
        1 egg, lightly beaten
    3/4 cup butter *or* margarine, melted
    1/4 cup sugar

In a large bowl, dissolve yeast in water; let stand for 5 minutes. Combine flour, egg, butter and sugar; add to yeast mixture and mix well. Fill greased or paper-lined muffin cups two-thirds full. Bake at 400° for 20-25 minutes or until muffins test done. **Yield:** 2-1/2 to 3 dozen.

BANANA PRALINE MUFFINS

Margaret Balley, Coffeeville, Mississippi

Ever since my children were small (and it became too difficult for Santa to transport his goods!), I've invited my parents and in-laws over for Christmas breakfast. Undoubtedly, part of the tradition included these easy, rich muffins.

    1/3 cup chopped pecans

        3 tablespoons brown sugar
        1 tablespoon sour cream
        1 egg, lightly beaten
        3 small ripe bananas, mashed (about 1 cup)
    1/2 cup sugar
    1/4 cup vegetable oil
  1-1/2 cups packaged pancake mix

In a small bowl, combine pecans, brown sugar and sour cream; set aside. Combine egg, bananas, sugar and oil; mix well. Stir in pancake mix just until moistened. Fill greased or paper-lined muffin cups two-thirds full. Drop 1 teaspoon of pecan mixture into center of each muffin. Bake at 400° for 15-20 minutes or until muffins test done. **Yield:** about 1 dozen.

LEFTOVER SQUASH MUFFINS

Norma Hutchinson, Marion, Michigan

When I found this recipe in a magazine and adapted it to my taste, it quickly became a family favorite. By canning half-pints of squash in the summer, I'm able to make these all winter long!

        3 cups all-purpose flour
        1 cup sugar
        4 teaspoons baking powder
        1 teaspoon salt
        1 teaspoon ground cinnamon
    3/4 to 1 teaspoon ground nutmeg
        1 cup milk
        1 cup pureed cooked winter squash
    1/2 cup butter *or* margarine, softened
        2 eggs, lightly beaten

In a large bowl, combine first six ingredients; mix well. In a separate bowl, combine milk, squash, butter and eggs; stir into dry ingredients just until moistened. Fill greased or paper-lined muffin cups two-thirds full. Bake at 350° for 20-22 minutes. **Yield:** about 1-1/2 dozen.

FEATHER-LIGHT BREAKFAST PUFFS

Tina Christensen, Addison, Illinois

Don't let the stiff batter of these muffins fool you; these slightly sweet puffs really bake up light and delicate. Serve them hot and they'll melt in your mouth!

    1/3 cup shortening
        1 egg
  1-1/2 cups all-purpose flour
    1/2 cup sugar
  1-1/2 teaspoons baking powder
    1/2 teaspoon salt
    1/4 teaspoon ground nutmeg
    1/2 cup milk
  TOPPING:
    1/2 cup sugar
        1 teaspoon ground cinnamon
        6 tablespoons butter *or* margarine, melted

In a mixing bowl, beat shortening and egg. Combine the flour, sugar, baking powder, salt and nutmeg. Stir into egg mixture alternately with milk (batter will be stiff). Fill greased or paper-lined muffin cups two-thirds full. Bake at 350° for 15-20 minutes or muffins test done. For topping, combine sugar and cinnamon. When puffs are removed from the oven, immediately roll each in butter and then into cinnamon-sugar. Serve hot. **Yield:** about 1 dozen.

LOW-FAT LEMON POPPY SEED MUFFINS

Pam Williamson, Fort Worth, Texas

I enjoy trying new muffin recipes, so was I glad when I stumbled upon this one. The applesauce makes these lemon muffins so moist and delicious.

> 2-1/4 cups all-purpose flour
> 1-1/2 cups sugar
> 1/4 cup poppy seeds
> 1 tablespoon baking powder
> 3 eggs, lightly beaten *or* egg substitute equivalent
> 1-1/4 cups skim milk
> 3/4 cup applesauce
> 2 teaspoons lemon extract

In a large bowl, combine flour, sugar, poppy seeds and baking powder. Combine eggs, milk, applesauce and lemon extract; stir into dry ingredients just until moistened. Fill greased or paper-lined muffin cups three-fourths full. Bake at 350° for 30-35 minutes or until muffins test done. **Yield:** 1 to 1-1/2 dozen.

EARLY-RISER MUFFINS

Brenda Offutt, Lincoln, Nebraska

Despite the name, you don't have to be an early-riser to enjoy these hearty muffins (we often make them for brunch). My husband and children come running when they smell these buttery, tender muffins baking.

> 2 cups all-purpose flour
> 2 tablespoons sugar
> 1 tablespoon baking powder
> 1/2 teaspoon salt
> 1/4 teaspoon dry mustard
> 1 egg, lightly beaten
> 1 cup milk
> 1/3 cup butter *or* margarine, melted
> 3/4 cup finely chopped ham
> 3/4 cup shredded cheddar cheese

In a bowl, combine flour, sugar, baking powder, salt and mustard. Combine egg, milk and butter; stir into dry ingredients just until moistened. Fold in ham and cheese. Fill greased or paper-lined muffin cups two-thirds full. Bake at 400° for 20-25 minutes or until muffins test done. Cool in pan 10 minutes before removing to a wire rack. **Yield:** about 1 dozen.

CINNAMON-TOPPED RHUBARB MUFFINS

Joy Toso, Rothsay, Minnesota

I like to bake these tasty muffins fresh in the morning and share them with elderly neighbors who no longer bake for themselves. The farm where my husband and I live has been in my family for 110 years. In fact, I was born here!

> 2-1/2 cups all-purpose flour
> 1-1/2 cups packed brown sugar
> 1 teaspoon salt
> 1 teaspoon baking soda
> 1 teaspoon ground cinnamon
> 1 egg, lightly beaten
> 1 cup buttermilk
> 2/3 cup vegetable oil
> 1 teaspoon vanilla extract
> 2 cups finely chopped rhubarb
> TOPPING:
> 1/2 cup sugar
> 2 tablespoons butter *or* margarine, melted
> 2 teaspoons ground cinnamon

In a large bowl, combine the first five ingredients. Combine egg, buttermilk, oil and vanilla; stir into dry ingredients just until moistened. Fold in rhubarb. Fill greased or paper-lined muffin cups half full. Combine topping ingredients; sprinkle over each muffin. Bake at 375° for 16-18 minutes or until muffins test done. **Yield:** about 2 dozen.

STRAWBERRY STREUSEL MUFFINS

Mina Dyck, Boissevain, Manitoba

Muffins have always been a favorite breakfast food for my family. My children have now "left the nest", but I still find myself mixing a batch of these muffins using strawberries from my garden.

> 2-1/4 cups all-purpose flour
> 1/3 cup sugar
> 1 tablespoon baking powder
> 1/4 teaspoon salt
> 1-1/2 cups coarsely chopped fresh strawberries
> 2 eggs, lightly beaten
> 1/2 cup milk
> 1/2 cup sour cream
> 1/3 cup vegetable oil
> STREUSEL TOPPING:
> 1/4 cup all-purpose flour
> 1/4 cup packed brown sugar
> 1/2 teaspoon ground cinnamon
> 2 tablespoons cold butter *or* margarine

In a large bowl, combine flour, sugar, baking powder and salt. Gently fold in strawberries. Combine eggs, milk, sour cream and oil; stir into dry ingredients just until moistened. Fill greased or paper-lined muffin cups two-thirds full. For topping, combine flour, brown sugar and cinnamon; mix well. Cut in butter until crumbly. Sprinkle about 2-1/2 teaspoons over each muffin. Bake at 425° for 20-25 minutes or until muffins test done. Cool in pan 10 minutes before removing to a wire rack. **Yield:** about 1 dozen.

PEACHY MOIST MUFFINS

Lisa Baker, Stromsburg, Nebraska
(PICTURED AT LEFT)

Whenever I make these, I always get compliments because of their sweet and tender texture. I'm sure your family will agree that these delicious muffins are just "peachy"!

1-1/2 cups all-purpose flour
   1 cup chopped pecans
   3/4 cup sugar
1-1/2 teaspoons baking powder
   1 egg, lightly beaten
   1/2 cup peach *or* vanilla yogurt
   1/2 cup butter *or* margarine, melted
   1 teaspoon vanilla extract
   1 cup chopped peeled fresh *or* well-drained
      canned peaches

In a large bowl, combine flour, pecans, sugar and baking powder. Combine egg, yogurt, butter and vanilla; mix well. Stir into dry ingredients just until moistened. Fold in peaches. Fill greased or paper-lined muffin cups two-thirds full. Bake at 400° for 15-20 minutes or until muffins test done. Cool in pan 10 minutes before removing to a wire rack. **Yield:** about 1 dozen.

LEMON/RASPBERRY STREUSEL MUFFINS

Marie Herr, Berea, Ohio
(PICTURED AT LEFT)

Fresh from the oven, these attractive, delicious muffins make a great accompaniment to any breakfast or brunch. I usually double the recipe because they seem to disappear the minute I put them out.

   2 cups all-purpose flour
   1/2 cup sugar
   2 teaspoons baking powder
   1/2 teaspoon baking soda
   1/2 teaspoon salt
   2 eggs, lightly beaten
   1 cup (8 ounces) lemon yogurt
   1/2 cup vegetable oil
   1 teaspoon grated lemon peel
   1 cup fresh *or* frozen raspberries
TOPPING:
   1/3 cup sugar
   1/4 cup all-purpose flour
   2 tablespoons butter *or* margarine

In a large bowl, combine flour, sugar, baking powder, baking soda and salt. Combine eggs, yogurt, oil and lemon peel; mix well. Stir into dry ingredients just until moistened.

> **HOMEMADE GOODIES.** *Pictured at left, clockwise from the bottom: Lemon/Raspberry Streusel Muffins, Peachy Moist Muffins and Blueberry Cornmeal Muffins (all recipes on this page).*

Fold in raspberries. Fill greased or paper-lined muffin cups three-fourths full. For topping, combine sugar and flour. Cut in butter until mixture resembles coarse crumbs; sprinkle about 1 tablespoon over each muffin. Bake at 400° for 18-20 minutes or until muffins test done. Cool in pan 10 minutes before removing to a wire rack. **Yield:** about 1 dozen.

BLUEBERRY CORNMEAL MUFFINS

Betsy Faye Steenbock, Shoshoni, Wyoming
(PICTURED AT LEFT)

When our daughter Lisa was growing up, she was always eager to help me cook, especially sweets! When her father came in for a late brunch after working hard in the fields, she loved to have these made-from-scratch muffins waiting for him.

1-1/4 cups all-purpose flour
   3/4 cup cornmeal
   1/4 cup sugar
   2 teaspoons baking powder
   1/2 teaspoon salt
   1 cup fresh *or* frozen blueberries
   1 cup milk
   1/4 cup vegetable oil
   2 egg whites

In a large bowl, combine flour, cornmeal, sugar, baking powder and salt. Add blueberries. Stir in milk and oil just until mixed. In a mixing bowl, beat egg whites until stiff peaks form; fold into batter. Fill greased or paper-lined muffin cups two-thirds full. Bake at 400° for 20-25 minutes or until muffins test done. **Yield:** about 1 dozen.

NEW YORK STATE MUFFINS

Beverly Collins, North Syracuse, New York

These hearty muffins are packed with so many tasty ingredients that they make a great breakfast just by themselves. Or serve them with fresh fruit and ham for a complete hearty meal.

2-1/2 cups all-purpose flour
1-1/3 cups sugar
   1 tablespoon baking powder
   2 teaspoons baking soda
   2 teaspoons ground cinnamon
   1/2 teaspoon salt
   2 eggs, lightly beaten
   1/2 cup vegetable oil
   2 cups finely chopped peeled apples
   1 cup shredded carrots
   1 cup whole cranberries
   1 cup chopped walnuts

In a large bowl, combine flour, sugar, baking powder, baking soda, cinnamon and salt. Mix eggs and oil. Add apples and carrots; stir into dry ingredients just until moistened (batter will be thick). Fold in cranberries and nuts. Fill greased or paper-lined muffin cups two-thirds full. Bake at 375° for 20-25 minutes or until muffins test done. **Yield:** about 1-1/2 dozen.

OATMEAL-CINNAMON MUFFINS

Coleen Roberts, Seffner, Florida

This is my favorite muffin recipe because it adapts so well to variations. To make these delicious muffins even more hearty, I sometimes add chopped apple, raisins or shredded carrots.

> 1 cup old-fashioned oats
> 1 cup buttermilk
> 2 eggs, lightly beaten
> 1 cup all-purpose flour
> 1/3 cup packed brown sugar
> 1-1/2 teaspoons baking powder
> 1 teaspoon ground cinnamon
> 1/2 teaspoon baking soda

In a large bowl, combine oats and buttermilk; let stand 5 minutes. Stir in eggs. Combine flour, brown sugar, baking powder, cinnamon and baking soda; stir into oatmeal mixture just until moistened. Fill greased or paper-lined muffin cups two-thirds full. Bake at 400° for 18-20 minutes or until muffins test done. Cool in pan 10 minutes before removing to a wire rack. **Yield:** 8-10 muffins.

NUTTY PUMPKIN MUFFINS

Denise Baumert, Jameson, Missouri

The medley of harvest flavors makes these muffins perfect for cool fall mornings. But my family enjoys them year-round, so I always have the ingredients on hand for fresh-from-the-oven goodness.

> 2 eggs, beaten
> 1-1/2 cups sugar
> 1 cup canned *or* cooked mashed pumpkin
> 1/2 cup vegetable oil
> 1/3 cup water
> 1-2/3 cups all-purpose flour
> 1 teaspoon ground cinnamon
> 1 teaspoon baking soda
> 1/2 teaspoon baking powder
> 1/2 teaspoon salt
> 3/4 cup chopped cashews *or* walnuts

In a large bowl, mix eggs, sugar, pumpkin, oil and water. Combine flour, cinnamon, baking soda, baking powder and salt. Stir into pumpkin mixture; mix well. Fold in nuts. Fill greased or paper-lined muffin cups three-fourths full. Bake at 350° for 20-25 minutes or until muffins test done. Do not overbake. Cool on wire rack. **Yield:** about 1 dozen.

EASY OAT BRAN MUFFINS

Pauline Schminke, Vinton, Iowa

When I want to make muffins in a hurry, this is the recipe I use. The oat bran cereal makes these easy to prepare, and the sweet dark molasses adds a rich flavor.

> 2 cups oat bran cereal
> 1/4 cup packed brown sugar

> 2 teaspoons baking powder
> 1 egg *or* 2 egg whites, lightly beaten
> 1 cup milk
> 1/4 cup dark molasses
> 2 tablespoons vegetable oil

In a large bowl, combine cereal, brown sugar and baking powder. Combine egg, milk, molasses and oil; mix well. Add to dry ingredients and stir just until moistened. Fill greased or paper-lined muffin cups three-fourths full. Bake at 425° for 15-17 minutes or until muffins test done. Cool in pan 10 minutes before removing to a wire rack. **Yield:** 8-10 muffins.

CRANBERRY-CARDAMOM MUFFINS

Linda Haney, Waterman, Illinois

This cranberry muffin recipe was handed down to me from my Swedish mother and grandmother, who liked using cardamom in almost anything! You'll enjoy the light cake-like texture.

> 3-1/2 cups all-purpose flour
> 1-3/4 cups sugar
> 1-3/4 teaspoons baking soda
> 1 teaspoon baking powder
> 1/2 teaspoon salt
> 1/2 teaspoon ground cardamom
> 1-1/2 cups fresh *or* frozen cranberries
> 4 eggs, lightly beaten
> 2 cups (16 ounces) sour cream
> 1/2 cup butter *or* margarine, melted
> 1 teaspoon vanilla extract

In a large bowl, combine flour, sugar, baking soda, baking powder, salt and cardamom. Add cranberries; stir to coat. In a small bowl, combine eggs, sour cream, butter and vanilla; mix well. Add to cranberry mixture; stir just until moistened. Fill greased or paper-lined muffin cups two-thirds full. Bake at 375° for 15-20 minutes or until muffins test done. Remove from pans; serve warm. **Yield:** about 2 dozen.

MORNING GLORY MUFFINS

Lorna Schwingle-Glass, Lomira, Wisconsin

I found this recipe for hearty muffins in a cookbook I received as a Christmas gift years ago. Now my family often requests that I make these, especially after we go apple-picking in fall.

> 4 cups all-purpose flour
> 2-1/2 cups sugar
> 4 teaspoons baking soda
> 4 teaspoons ground cinnamon
> 1 teaspoon salt
> 2 cups vegetable oil
> 6 eggs, lightly beaten
> 4 teaspoons vanilla extract
> 4 cups grated peeled apples
> 1 cup raisins
> 1 cup flaked coconut

1 cup shredded carrots
1 cup chopped walnuts

In a large bowl, combine flour, sugar, baking soda, cinnamon and salt. Mix oil, eggs and vanilla; stir into dry ingredients just until moistened. Fold in apples, raisins, coconut, carrots and nuts. Fill greased or paper-lined muffin cups two-thirds full. Bake at 350° for 25-30 minutes or until muffins test done. **Yield:** about 3 dozen.

HOME-STYLE CHEESE MUFFINS
Mina Dyck, Boissevain, Manitoba

These muffins are a savory addition to your favorite breakfast or brunch. My family loves them so much that I make sure to have some shredded cheese in the refrigerator so I can whip them up in a hurry.

    2 cups all-purpose flour
    1 tablespoon baking powder
1/2 teaspoon salt
    1 egg, lightly beaten
    1 cup milk
1/4 cup butter *or* margarine, melted
2/3 cup shredded cheddar cheese

In a bowl, combine flour, baking powder and salt. Mix egg, milk and butter; stir into dry ingredients just until moistened. Fold in cheese. Fill greased or paper-lined muffin cups two-thirds full. Bake at 400° for 20-25 minutes or until golden brown. **Yield:** about 1 dozen.

APPLE-FILLED CRANBERRY MUFFINS
Michele Bragg, Palm City, Florida

Now that I live in Florida, making these tasty muffins takes me back to my days in the Northeast, where cranberries and apples are in abundance.

FILLING:
1-1/2 cups finely chopped peeled apples
    2 tablespoons sugar
    1 teaspoon ground cinnamon
MUFFINS:
    3 cups all-purpose flour
    2 cups sugar
    3 teaspoons baking powder
    1 teaspoon salt
    4 eggs, lightly beaten
    1 cup vegetable oil
1/2 cup cranberry juice
1/2 cup finely chopped fresh cranberries
    3 tablespoons vanilla extract

For filling, combine apples, sugar and cinnamon; set aside. For muffins, combine flour, sugar, baking powder and salt. Combine eggs, oil, cranberry juice, cranberries and vanilla; stir into dry ingredients just until moistened. Fill greased or paper-lined muffin cups one-third full. Spoon 1 tablespoon filling on top. Fill muffin cups two-thirds full with remaining batter. Bake at 350° for 35-40 minutes or until muffins test done. Cool 10 minutes before removing to a wire rack. **Yield:** about 1-1/2 dozen. **Editor's Note:** 3 tablespoons of vanilla is correct.

ORANGE MUFFINS WITH DATES
Marion Morck, Spruce View, Alberta

I love preparing baked goods and sharing them with family and friends. These light yet flavorful muffins are always such a hit that I often end up sharing the recipe as well.

    1 orange
1/2 cup orange juice
    1 tablespoon grated orange peel
    1 egg
1/2 cup vegetable oil
    1 cup whole wheat flour
3/4 cup packed brown sugar
1/2 cup all-purpose flour
    1 teaspoon baking powder
    1 teaspoon baking soda
1/2 teaspoon salt
1/2 cup chopped dates

Peel orange, reserving peel, and separate orange into segments. Place peel, segments and juice in a blender or food processor. Add egg and oil; blend well. In a bowl, combine whole wheat flour, brown sugar, all-purpose flour, baking powder, baking soda and salt. Add orange mixture and stir just until moistened. Fold in dates. Fill greased or paper-lined muffin cups two-thirds full. Bake at 400° for 14-16 minutes or until muffins test done. **Yield:** about 1 dozen.

CRANBERRY YOGURT MUFFINS
Shari Johnson, Harmony, Maine

The use of yogurt instead of oil really makes these muffins moist. And the cranberries and orange peel provide lots of flavor. With such great taste, no one will ever guess that they're so easy to prepare!

1-1/2 cups all-purpose flour
3/4 cup sugar
    2 teaspoons baking powder
    1 teaspoon baking soda
1/8 teaspoon salt
2/3 cup nonfat plain yogurt
2/3 cup skim milk
    1 cup chopped cranberries
1/2 teaspoon grated orange peel

In a large bowl, combine flour, sugar, baking powder, baking soda and salt. Gently fold in yogurt and milk just until moistened. Stir in cranberries and orange peel. Fill greased or paper-lined muffin cups three-fourths full. Bake at 400° for 20-25 minutes or until muffins test done. **Yield:** about 1 dozen.

Cookin' Up...
SATISFYING CEREALS

Hot or cold, these hearty homemade cereals are not only easy to make, they're loaded with natural ingredients and unbeatable taste.

CRUNCHY BREAKFAST CEREAL

Carol Fischer, Pewaukee, Wisconsin
(PICTURED AT LEFT)

While I was growing up, my mom would often make this delicious sweet cereal. I loved it so much, I remember requesting it for breakfast, lunch and dinner!

   6 cups old-fashioned oats
   2 cups whole wheat flour
   2 cups packed brown sugar
   2 cups flaked coconut
1-1/2 cups chopped pecans
   1 cup wheat germ
   1 cup all-bran cereal
  3/4 cup vegetable oil
  3/4 cup water
   2 tablespoons vanilla extract
   1 teaspoon salt
   1 cup raisins

In a large bowl, combine oats, flour, brown sugar, coconut, pecans, wheat germ and cereal. In another bowl, mix oil, water, vanilla and salt. Pour over oat mixture; toss to coat. Pour into two greased 15-in. x 10-in. x 1-in. baking pans. Bake at 275° for 1 hour, stirring every 10 minutes. Add raisins. Store in an airtight container. **Yield:** 16 cups.

FRUIT 'N' NUT GRANOLA

Sue Hochhalter-Broyles, Rapelje, Montana
(PICTURED AT LEFT)

The combination of crunchy nut and chewy fruit makes this granola a hit for breakfast or for snacking. It's packed with lots of ingredients that taste great.

4 cups old-fashioned oats
1 cup nonfat dry milk powder
1 cup chopped dried mixed fruit
1/2 cup chopped walnuts
1/4 cup wheat germ
1 tablespoon ground cinnamon

HEARTY STARTERS. *Pictured at left, clockwise from the top: Fruit 'n' Nut Granola, Crunchy Breakfast Cereal (in jar and bowl) and Muesli (all recipes on this page).*

3/4 cup packed brown sugar
1/4 cup water
1/2 cup vegetable oil
  1 teaspoon vanilla extract
1/2 cup raisins

In a large bowl, combine oats, milk powder, fruit, walnuts, wheat germ and cinnamon. In a saucepan over medium heat, bring brown sugar and water to a boil. Remove from the heat; stir in oil and vanilla until mixed. Pour over oat mixture and toss to coat. Pour into a greased 15-in. x 10-in. x 1-in. baking pan. Bake at 275° for 1 hour and 30 minutes or until golden brown, stirring every 15 minutes. Stir in raisins. Cool, stirring occasionally. Store in an airtight container. **Yield:** 7 cups.

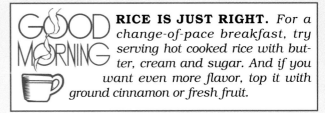

RICE IS JUST RIGHT. *For a change-of-pace breakfast, try serving hot cooked rice with butter, cream and sugar. And if you want even more flavor, top it with ground cinnamon or fresh fruit.*

MUESLI

Ann Belczak, North Tonawanda, New York
(PICTURED AT LEFT)

I received this authentic recipe from a New Zealand pen pal. My family loves the naturally sweet flavor of the honey, and I like it because it's not loaded with preservatives.

   6 cups old-fashioned oats
1-1/2 cups wheat germ
1-1/2 cups all-bran cereal
  1/2 cup flaked coconut
1-1/2 cups honey
  1/2 cup chopped walnuts
  1/2 cup chopped dried apricots

In a large bowl, combine oats, wheat germ, cereal and coconut. Pour into two greased 13-in. x 9-in. x 2-in. baking pans. Bake at 275° for 20 minutes, stirring once. Heat honey in a saucepan until thin, about 5 minutes. Pour half into each pan; stir to coat evenly. Return to the oven for 20-30 minutes or until golden, stirring every 10 minutes. Stir in walnuts and apricots. Cool, stirring occasionally. Store in an airtight container. **Yield:** 11 cups.

GOLDEN CINNAMON GRANOLA

Marilyn Dick, Centralia, Missouri

This basic granola recipe is a must to have on hand at our house. With a great cinnamon flavor, it's perfect for a quick and hearty breakfast or snack.

- 1/4 cup butter *or* margarine, melted
- 1/4 cup honey
- 1-1/2 teaspoons ground cinnamon
- 1/2 teaspoon salt
- 3 cups old-fashioned oats
- 1 cup flaked coconut
- 1 cup chopped walnuts
- 2/3 cup raisins

In a bowl, stir butter, honey, cinnamon and salt until well blended. Combine the oats, coconut and walnuts in a greased 13-in. x 9-in. x 2-in. baking pan. Add butter mixture and stir to coat evenly. Bake at 275° for 50-60 minutes or until golden brown, stirring every 15 minutes. Add raisins. Cool, stirring occasionally. Store in an airtight container. **Yield:** about 7 cups.

BUTTERSCOTCH OATMEAL

Janet Nielsen, New Brighton, Minnesota

My husband and I look forward to a hot bowl of oatmeal on cold winter mornings. This sweet version of oatmeal is so good we could eat it almost every day!

- 1-3/4 cups milk
- 1/2 cup packed brown sugar
- 1 egg, lightly beaten
- 1 cup quick-cooking oats
- 1 tablespoon butter *or* margarine

In a saucepan over medium heat, combine milk, brown sugar and egg. Cook, stirring constantly, for 5-7 minutes or until mixture boils. Add oats; cook and stir for 1 minute. Remove from the heat. Add butter; cover and let stand for 3-5 minutes. **Yield:** 3-4 servings.

OVERNIGHT BAKED PORRIDGE

Vi Kuhns, Elkhart, Indiana

I've always loved to cook. And coming from a family of seven brothers and three sisters, there was always someone willing to be my "guinea pig"! I still like to try new recipes, but this tried-and-true dish is one of my favorites.

- 4-1/2 cups water
- 3 cups quick-cooking oats
- 2 eggs, lightly beaten
- 2 apples, peeled and chopped (about 1 cup)
- 1 cup packed brown sugar
- 1/2 cup milk
- 1/2 cup vegetable oil
- 1/2 cup raisins
- 2 teaspoons baking powder

- 1 teaspoon salt
- 1/2 teaspoon ground cinnamon
- Additional milk, optional

In a saucepan, bring water to a boil; add oats. Return to a boil; cook 1 minute. Remove from the heat; cover and let stand for 5 minutes. Combine eggs, apples, brown sugar, milk, oil, raisins, baking powder, salt and cinnamon. Stir in oatmeal. Spoon into a greased 9-in. square baking pan. Cover and refrigerate overnight. Remove from refrigerator 30 minutes before baking. Bake, uncovered, at 350° for 60-65 minutes or until a knife inserted near the center comes out clean. Cut into squares; pour milk over each serving if desired. **Yield:** 9 servings.

ORANGE BREAKFAST CRUNCH TOPPING

Mrs. Rufus Engle, Bonita Springs, Florida

I always find oatmeal to be a little plain for my tastes, but this unique topping really adds some character. I've been interested in cooking as long as I can remember...I even made my own wedding cake some 67 years ago!

- 1-1/2 cups wheat germ
- 1 tablespoon grated orange peel
- 1/2 teaspoon ground cinnamon
- 1/2 cup packed brown sugar
- 1/4 cup butter *or* margarine

In a greased 8-in. square baking dish, mix wheat germ, orange peel and cinnamon; set aside. In a saucepan, heat brown sugar and butter until butter is melted. Pour over wheat germ mixture; stir to coat. Bake at 275° for 20-30 minutes or until browned, stirring every 10 minutes. Cool, stirring occasionally. Store, covered, in refrigerator. Serve over oatmeal, fruit or waffles. **Yield:** 2-1/2 cups.

NOT JUST FOR BREAKFAST. *Served with hot or cold milk, granola is a tasty, filling breakfast. But it also makes a great anytime snack, either alone or sprinkled over fresh fruit, yogurt... even ice cream!*

HONEY COCONUT GRANOLA

Lois Van Dusseldorp, Platte, South Dakota

Getting kids to eat anything for breakfast can often be a challenge. But one taste of this slightly sweet granola and they'll be hooked!

- 15 cups old-fashioned oats (about 3 pounds)
- 1 cup chopped walnuts
- 1 cup wheat germ
- 1 cup sunflower seeds
- 1 bag (14 ounces) flaked coconut
- 1 cup butter *or* margarine

1 cup packed brown sugar
1 cup honey
1/2 cup vegetable oil
1 tablespoon vanilla extract
1 tablespoon maple flavoring
1/2 teaspoon salt
1 cup raisins, optional

In a large bowl, combine oats, walnuts, wheat germ, sunflower seeds and coconut. In a saucepan over medium heat, stir butter, brown sugar, honey, oil, flavorings and salt until well mixed. Pour over oat mixture and stir to coat evenly. Pour into three greased 13-in. x 9-in. x 2-in. baking pans. Bake at 275° for 60-70 minutes or until golden brown, stirring every 15 minutes. Add raisins if desired. Cool, stirring occasionally. Store in an airtight container. **Yield:** 21 cups.

BAKED OATMEAL SQUARES
Elaine Heckman, Bechtelsville, Pennsylvania

This quick and easy Amish breakfast bar recipe is one of my most cherished because it's hearty and flavorful. My wonderful husband loves to eat...especially what I make!

1 egg, lightly beaten
1-1/2 cups quick-cooking oats
1/2 cup sugar
1/2 cup milk
1/4 cup vegetable oil
1/4 cup chopped nuts
1/4 cup raisins
1 teaspoon baking powder
1/2 teaspoon salt
1/2 teaspoon ground cinnamon

Combine all ingredients in a bowl. Pour into a greased 8-in. square baking dish. Bake at 350° for 25 minutes. Cut into squares. **Yield:** 4-6 servings.

SPICED DATE OATMEAL
Patricia Kaliska, Phillips, Wisconsin

You can prepare this hearty oatmeal in a hurry. And if you don't have dates available, try substituting raisins. Everyone will love this filling dish.

2 cups apple juice
1 cup quick-cooking oats
1/2 cup chopped dates
1/4 teaspoon ground cinnamon

Dash ground nutmeg
Milk
Coconut, optional

In a saucepan, bring apple juice to a boil. Stir in oats; cook 1 minute. Remove from the heat; stir in dates, cinnamon and nutmeg. Cover and let stand for 5 minutes. Serve with milk and sprinkle with coconut if desired. **Yield:** 2 servings.

PEAR-OATMEAL BREAKFAST PUDDING
Joyce Robbins, Old Hickory, Tennessee

No one will be able to refuse this sweet and tasty variation of oatmeal. Have plenty prepared...they may ask for seconds!

1 can (29 ounces) pear halves
2 cups milk
2 tablespoons brown sugar, *divided*
1 tablespoon butter *or* margarine
1/4 teaspoon salt
1/4 teaspoon ground cinnamon
1-1/2 cups old-fashioned oats
1/4 cup raisins
Light cream *or* additional milk

Drain pears, reserving 1 cup syrup in a saucepan. Set pears aside. To the syrup, add milk, 1 tablespoon brown sugar, butter, salt and cinnamon; heat until simmering. Dice all but two pear halves; stir into syrup mixture. Add oats and raisins. Heat until bubbly. Pour into a greased 1-1/2-qt. baking dish. Bake at 350° for 20 minutes; stir. Slice remaining pear halves; arrange over top. Sprinkle with remaining brown sugar. Bake 10-15 minutes longer. Serve hot with cream or milk. **Yield:** 6 servings.

CRISPY BREAKFAST SLICES
Dorothy Knowles, East Hampton, New York

I often prepared this dish when my kids were young. Now that they're grown, I still make it for my husband. He finally admits he looked forward to eating it as much as the kids!

3 cups water
1/4 cup sugar
1 teaspoon salt
1/2 teaspoon ground cinnamon
1/2 teaspoon ground nutmeg
2 cups quick-cooking oats
Butter *or* margarine
Maple syrup, optional

In a saucepan, bring water, sugar, salt, cinnamon and nutmeg to a boil. Stir in oats. Return to a boil; cook 1 minute. Remove from the heat; cover and let stand for 5 minutes. Pour into a greased 8-1/2-in. x 4-1/2-in. x 2-1/2-in. loaf pan. Cover and refrigerate overnight. Unmold and cut into 1/2-in. slices. Fry in butter in a skillet over medium heat until browned, about 6-8 minutes. Serve with syrup if desired. **Yield:** 8 servings.

HONEY CEREAL BITES

Sarah Carpenter, Trumansburg, New York

A neighbor lady gave me this recipe years ago, and my husband and kids immediately loved it. We have fun varying the recipe to add our own personal touches.

6 cups puffed wheat cereal
2 cups salted peanuts
1/4 cup sesame seeds, toasted
1/2 cup packed brown sugar
1/4 cup honey
1/4 cup butter *or* margarine

In a large bowl, combine cereal, peanuts and sesame seeds. In a small saucepan over low heat, cook brown sugar, honey and butter, stirring frequently until smooth. Pour over cereal mixture and toss to coat. Spread in two ungreased 13-in. x 9-in. x 2-in. baking pans. Bake at 275° for 45 minutes, stirring every 15 minutes. Cool. Store in an airtight container. **Yield:** 9-10 cups.

VANILLA GRANOLA

Elsie Beachy, Plain City, Ohio

This recipe was given to me by my aunt, who often prepared it for her own family. My family just loves the vanilla flavor and the sesame seeds.

6 cups quick-cooking oats
1 cup chopped walnuts
1/2 cup flaked coconut
1/2 cup sesame seeds
2/3 cup vegetable oil
1/2 cup honey
1/2 cup packed brown sugar
2 tablespoons water
1-1/2 teaspoons vanilla extract

In a large bowl, toss oats, walnuts, coconut and sesame seeds. In a saucepan over medium heat, cook oil, honey, brown sugar, water and vanilla until well mixed. Pour over oat mixture and stir to coat evenly. Pour into two greased 13-in. x 9-in. x 2-in. baking pans. Bake at 275° for 50-60 minutes or until golden brown, stirring every 15 minutes. Cool, stirring occasionally. Store in an airtight container. **Yield:** 8 cups.

OATMEAL WITH APPLES

Amie Jaramillo, Interlaken, New York

My twin girls can give me double trouble when I try to feed them breakfast. But whenever I make this recipe, they always have big helpings. They also like to help pick the apples from the trees in our own backyard.

1 apple, peeled and finely diced
2-1/3 cups apple juice
1-1/3 cups quick-cooking oats
1 teaspoon ground cinnamon
1/2 teaspoon salt
2 to 3 tablespoons raisins

2 teaspoons honey
1 teaspoon vanilla extract

In a saucepan, combine apple, apple juice, oats, cinnamon and salt. Bring to a boil; boil for 1 minute, stirring occasionally. Remove from the heat; stir in raisins, honey and vanilla. Cover and let stand for 5 minutes. **Yield:** 3-4 servings.

CHOCOLATE-OAT GRANOLA

Jane Driscoll, Sarasota, Florida

My husband and I sampled this granola years ago when we were overnight guests at a friend's house. It really appealed to our sweet tooth. She shared the recipe and I've been making it ever since.

6 cups old-fashioned oats
1 cup wheat germ
1 cup all-bran cereal
1 cup cornmeal
2 cups peanut butter
1 cup honey
1 cup chopped dried apples
1 cup golden raisins
1 cup (6 ounces) semisweet chocolate chips
1 cup sunflower seeds

In a large bowl, mix oats, wheat germ, cereal and cornmeal. In a saucepan over medium heat, cook peanut butter and honey until smooth and thin, about 5-8 minutes. Pour over oat mixture, stirring to coat evenly. Place in two greased 13-in. x 9-in. x 2-in. baking pans; bake at 275° for 60-70 minutes or until golden brown, stirring every 15 minutes. Cool, stirring occasionally. Add apples, raisins, chocolate chips and sunflower seeds. Store in an airtight container. **Yield:** 14-15 cups.

HOMEMADE GRAPE NUTS

Martha Barkman, Bird in Hand, Pennsylvania

I began making this recipe to save on cereal costs for our family of six. Everyone loves the hearty flavor that just can't be found in packaged cereals.

7 cups whole wheat flour
3 cups packed brown sugar
2-1/4 teaspoons baking soda
1 teaspoon salt
2-1/2 cups buttermilk
6 tablespoons butter *or* margarine, melted
2 teaspoons vanilla extract
1/2 teaspoon maple flavoring, optional
Milk

In a large bowl, combine flour, brown sugar, baking soda and salt. Add buttermilk, butter, vanilla and maple flavoring if desired, stirring until well mixed. Spread into six greased 13-in. x 9-in. x 2-in. baking pans. Bake at 350° for 35-40 minutes. Cool. Break into pieces and process in batches in a food processor until pieces are small. Return to baking pans and bake at 250° for 1 hour, stirring every 15 minutes, or until light brown and crisp. Serve as a cereal with milk. Store in an airtight container. **Yield:** 20 cups.

HOT CINNAMON WHEAT CEREAL

Michelle Bently, Niceville, Florida

Here's a quick warm breakfast for mornings when there's a chill in the air. For variety, we often top it with a spoonful of our favorite fruit preserves.

    1 large shredded wheat biscuit
    1 cup milk, warmed
Ground cinnamon to taste
Sugar to taste
    1 tablespoon butter *or* margarine

Place biscuit in a serving bowl; add milk. Sprinkle with cinnamon and sugar. Dot with butter. Serve immediately. **Yield:** 1 serving.

PEANUT BUTTER-HONEY BARS

Janet Hamacher, La Moille, Illinois

If you're in a hurry in the morning, just one of these bars with a glass of milk gets you started on the right foot. And if you have a hungry crew to feed, the recipe can be easily doubled.

    1/2 cup peanut butter
    2 eggs, lightly beaten
    1/4 cup honey
    2/3 cup nonfat dry milk powder
    3 cups fruit and fiber cereal (any flavor)

In a medium bowl, stir peanut butter, eggs and honey until smooth. Blend in milk powder. Add cereal and mix well. Spread in a greased 8-in. square baking pan. Bake at 325° for 20 minutes (mixture may look damp). Cool and cut into bars. Store in the refrigerator. **Yield:** 6 servings.

MIXED GRAIN AND WILD RICE CEREAL

Julie Capell, Milwaukee, Wisconsin

My husband and I love this flavorful cereal so much that I often prepare a large batch on weekends. Then on hurried weekday mornings, I simply reheat it.

    8 cups water, *divided*
    1/2 cup uncooked wild rice, rinsed
    1/2 cup pearl barley
    1/2 cup old-fashioned oats
    1/2 cup raisins
    1/2 cup chopped dates
    1/3 cup packed brown sugar
    3 tablespoons butter *or* margarine
    1/2 teaspoon ground cinnamon
Honey, optional

In a saucepan, combine 2 cups water and wild rice; bring to a boil. Cover and simmer for 20 minutes; drain. Place in a greased 2-1/2-qt. casserole; add the barley, oats, raisins, dates, brown sugar, butter, cinnamon and remaining water. Cover and bake at 375° for 1 hour and 40 minutes or until grains are tender, stirring occasionally. Serve warm with honey if desired. **Yield:** 8-10 servings.

BAKED APPLE OATMEAL

DeAnn Alleva, Charlotte, North Carolina

On cold winter mornings in Wisconsin, Mom warmed us up by serving this deliciously sweet cereal. Winters are mild here in North Carolina, but this oatmeal is still one of my favorites.

    4 cups milk
    1/2 cup packed brown sugar
    2 teaspoons butter *or* margarine
    1/2 teaspoon salt
    1/2 teaspoon ground cinnamon
    2 cups old-fashioned oats
    2 cups chopped peeled apples
    1 cup chopped walnuts
    1 cup raisins
    1 cup wheat germ

In a saucepan, heat milk, brown sugar, butter, salt and cinnamon. Add remaining ingredients; mix gently. Spoon into a greased 2-qt. casserole. Cover and bake at 350° for 45 minutes. **Yield:** 6-8 servings.

FRIED SHREDDED WHEAT

Barbara VanSlyke, Verona, New York

Intent on giving her family a hearty breakfast during the Depression, my mother-in-law came up with this simple recipe. With it's great flavor, this unique breakfast survived the generations and is now a favorite meal for my family.

    4 large shredded wheat biscuits
    3/4 cup milk
Maple syrup

Soak cereal in milk for 5 minutes on each side. Remove with a slotted spoon; drain slightly. Fry in a greased skillet until brown on both sides, pressing down while frying. Serve with syrup. **Yield:** 4 servings.

BANANA NUT MUESLI

Janet Dorfman, San Francisco, California

Although I love the flavor of homemade cereals, I rarely have time to make them from scratch. But this cereal is so wonderful not only because it's tasty...it's made the night before!

    1 cup water
    2/3 cup quick-cooking oats
    1 firm banana, sliced
    1/4 cup raisins
    1/4 cup chopped almonds
    1/4 teaspoon ground cinnamon

In a bowl, mix all of the ingredients. Cover and refrigerate overnight. Serve chilled. **Yield:** 2 servings.

Cookin' Up...
FRUITS & BEVERAGES

Pack some punch into your breakfast by whipping up a thirst-quenching beverage. And for a naturally sweet addition to any breakfast, try a refreshing fruit dish.

SPICED PEARS

Sue Fisher, Northfield Falls, Vermont
(PICTURED AT LEFT)

I try to serve a fruit dish with every breakfast to get some extra vitamins in our diet. Not only are these pears quick and easy to prepare, they're delicious!

- 1 can (16 ounces) pear halves
- 1/3 cup packed brown sugar
- 3/4 teaspoon ground nutmeg
- 3/4 teaspoon ground cinnamon

Drain pears, reserving syrup; set the pears aside. Place syrup, brown sugar, nutmeg and cinnamon in a saucepan. Bring to a boil. Reduce heat and simmer, uncovered, for 5 minutes, stirring frequently. Add pears and simmer about 5 minutes more or until heated through. **Yield:** 4 servings.

MARY'S BAKED FRUIT

Mary Neville, Fredericktown, Missouri
(PICTURED AT LEFT)

My family first sampled baked fruit years ago while dining out. They liked it so much I decided to create my own version. The result was this attractive and tasty dish.

- 1 can (16 ounces) apricot halves, drained
- 1 can (16 ounces) pear halves, drained
- 1 can (30 ounces) whole plums, drained, halved and pitted
- 1 can (29 ounces) peach halves, drained
- 1 can (8 ounces) pineapple slices, undrained
- 1/3 cup packed brown sugar
- 1 tablespoon butter *or* margarine
- 1/2 teaspoon ground cinnamon
- 1/4 teaspoon ground cloves

In a greased 13-in. x 9-in. x 2-in. baking pan, starting at a 9-in. end, arrange rows of fruit in the following order: half of the apricots, pears and plums, all of the peaches, then remaining apricots, pears and plums. Drain pineapple, reserving 1/2 cup of juice. Lay pineapple over fruit in pan. In a saucepan, combine the pineapple juice, brown

sugar, butter, cinnamon and cloves. Cook and stir until sugar is dissolved and butter is melted. Pour over fruit. Bake, uncovered, at 350° for 20-25 minutes or until heated through. **Yield:** 12-16 servings.

PEACH BREAKFAST SLUSH

Karen Hamilton, Ludington, Michigan
(PICTURED AT LEFT)

This refreshing beverage is a favorite of mine to serve at our many brunch get-togethers. Because it's made ahead of time, I can avoid the last-minute rush before the guests arrive.

- 1 can (16 ounces) sliced peaches, drained
- 1 can (6 ounces) frozen orange juice concentrate, thawed
- 1-1/2 cups apricot nectar
- 2 cups chilled lemon-lime soda

In a blender, combine peaches, orange juice and nectar; blend until smooth. Pour into a freezer container; cover and freeze until firm. To serve, scoop 2/3 cup frozen mixture into a glass; add 1/3 cup soda. **Yield:** 6 servings.

OVERNIGHT FRUIT CUP

Lois Dethloff, Amboy, Minnesota

I can't begin to count how many times I've been asked for this recipe...it's become my trademark! It's so simple because it's prepared the night before, giving me time to enjoy my mornings.

- 1 package (3 ounces) lemon-flavored gelatin
- 2 cups boiling water
- 1 can (6 ounces) frozen orange juice concentrate, thawed
- 1 can (20 ounces) pineapple chunks, undrained
- 1 can (16 ounces) sliced peaches, drained
- 1 can (11 ounces) mandarin orange segments, undrained
- 1 cup sliced fresh strawberries
- 1 cup fresh blueberries
- 1 cup green grapes
- 1 firm banana, thinly sliced

In a large bowl, dissolve gelatin in water. Add orange juice; mix well. Add all of the fruit; mix well. Cover and refrigerate overnight. **Yield:** 15-20 servings.

FRESH AND FRUITY. *Pictured at left, clockwise from the bottom: Spiced Pears, Mary's Baked Fruit and Peach Breakfast Slush (all recipes on this page).*

CINNAMON-HONEY GRAPEFRUIT

Mrs. Carson Sadler, Souris, Manitoba
(PICTURED AT RIGHT)

Naturally delicious grapefruit gains even more great flavor in this recipe. I often like to prepare this as a light breakfast. But it also makes an appealing addition to your morning meal.

1 grapefruit, halved
2 teaspoons honey
Dash ground cinnamon

Place grapefruit halves, cut side up, in an ovenproof pan. Loosen grapefruit sections. Drizzle each half with 1 teaspoon honey; sprinkle with cinnamon. Broil 2-3 minutes or until bubbly. Serve warm. **Yield:** 2 servings.

HOT CRANBERRY DRINK

Lory Scott, Stafford, Kansas
(PICTURED AT RIGHT)

My mother would brew a batch of this hot drink when any of us children were sick. One sip and we'd instantly feel better! Now I make it for my husband and daughter on dreary winter mornings or anytime they're feeling under the weather.

2 cups fresh *or* frozen cranberries
6 cups water, *divided*
1 cup sugar
1/4 cup red-hot candies
7 whole cloves
1/2 cup fresh orange juice
1/4 cup fresh lemon juice

In a saucepan, cook cranberries in 2 cups water until they pop. Strain through a fine sieve, reserving juice and discarding skins; set aside. In a large saucepan, combine sugar, candies, cloves and remaining water. Cook until candies are dissolved. Add orange and lemon juices and reserved cranberry juice; heat through. Remove cloves. Serve hot. **Yield:** 6-8 servings (about 2 quarts).

MANDARIN ORANGE SALAD

Cindy Ziliak, Evansville, Indiana
(PICTURED AT RIGHT)

This quick and colorful dish is perfect for family breakfasts. By preparing it ahead of time, I can enjoy many other activities such as cross-stitching, painting, reading and, most importantly, spending time with my three boys!

1 can (20 ounces) pineapple chunks
1 can (15 ounces) mandarin orange segments
1 package (3 ounces) tapioca pudding mix
1 package (3 ounces) cook and serve vanilla pudding mix
1 jar (6 ounces) maraschino cherries, drained
2 medium firm bananas, sliced

Drain pineapple and oranges, reserving juices; set fruit aside. Add water to juices to equal 3 cups; pour into a saucepan. Add pudding mixes; cook over medium-high heat, stirring constantly until thickened and bubbly, 5-10 minutes. Remove from the heat; cool. Place pineapple, oranges and cherries in a 2-qt. bowl; pour dressing over and stir to coat. Chill for several hours. Add bananas just before serving. **Yield:** 6-8 servings.

APPLE PIE A LA MODE SHAKE

Tina Wilson, Panama City, Florida

As a mother of a toddler, I'm always looking for good tasting yet nutritious treats. This shake complements any breakfast and also makes a great snack. In addition to cooking, my hobbies include gardening, crafting and painting.

1 cup plain nonfat yogurt
1/2 cup applesauce, frozen
2 tablespoons brown sugar
1/2 teaspoon ground cinnamon
1/2 teaspoon vanilla extract

Combine all ingredients in a blender until smooth. **Yield:** 1-2 servings (1-1/2 cups).

SLUSH FRUIT CUPS

Lynn Schumacher, Grant, Nebraska

I try to have some of these fruit cups in the freezer all the time so I can serve them to my family for breakfast or to unexpected company at any time of the day. The refreshing flavor and pretty color add a festive flair to any table.

1 can (20 ounces) crushed pineapple
1 package (10 ounces) frozen strawberries in juice, thawed
1 can (6 ounces) frozen orange juice concentrate, thawed
1 can (6 ounces) frozen lemonade concentrate, thawed
3 firm bananas, cut into 1/4-inch slices
1-1/2 cups lemon-lime soda
1 cup water
1 cup sugar
20 paper cups (5 ounces)

In a large bowl, mix pineapple, strawberries, orange juice, lemonade, bananas, soda, water and sugar. Pour about 1/2 cup into each paper cup. Cover with foil and freeze until firm. Remove from freezer 15 minutes before serving. Serve in a dessert cup. **Yield:** 20 servings (9-1/2 cups). **Editor's Note:** For 30 servings, pour by 1/3 cupfuls into paper-lined muffin cups.

SUNNY SELECTIONS. *Pictured at right, clockwise from the bottom: Cinnamon-Honey Grapefruit, Hot Cranberry Drink and Mandarin Orange Salad (all recipes on this page).*

BANANA SMOOTHIE

Ro Ann Cox, Lenoir, North Carolina

This has to be one of my favorite recipes because it can be made in a flash, yet it's full of flavor. I think the honey adds just the right amount of sweetness. Everyone will love it...not just banana lovers!

    2 cups milk
    2 medium ripe bananas
    1/4 cup honey
    1/2 teaspoon vanilla extract

Combine all ingredients in a blender until smooth. **Yield:** 3-4 servings (3-1/2 cups).

FRUITY BREAKFAST BEVERAGE

Debbie Rohler, Indianapolis, Indiana

This drink is a real winner. My husband had this recipe before we were married, and now it's one of our favorites. I especially like to serve this to guests because it's so pretty and tasty.

    2 cups orange juice
    1 frozen banana, quartered
    1/2 cup unsweetened frozen strawberries
    1/2 cup unsweetened frozen raspberries
    1 teaspoon honey

Combine all ingredients in a blender until smooth. Pour into glasses. **Yield:** 3-4 servings (3-1/2 cups).

HOT COCOA MIX

Danette Rogers, Greenville, South Carolina

My mother often had this mix on hand when I was growing up. Now I make this hot cocoa for my kids on cold and rainy mornings. It's cheaper than store-bought mixes and even more delicious.

    12 cups nonfat dry milk powder (2 pounds)
    1 pound confectioners' sugar
    1 container (16 ounces) chocolate milk mix
    1 jar (6 ounces) nondairy coffee creamer
    1/2 teaspoon salt

Mix all ingredients in a very large bowl. Store in an airtight container. To serve, mix 1/3 cup mix with 1 cup boiling water. **Yield:** 50 servings.

ORANGE-PECAN BAKED APPLES

Dorothy Pritchett, Wills Point, Texas

These deliciously filled baked apples make a fruitful finale to any breakfast. And you'll be happy to know they're easy to prepare.

    6 medium baking apples, cored
    1/4 cup orange marmalade

    2 tablespoons finely chopped pecans
Ground cinnamon
Ground nutmeg

Place apples in a shallow ungreased baking pan; add a small amount of water to pan. In a small bowl, combine marmalade and pecans; mix well. Fill center of apples with marmalade mixture; sprinkle with cinnamon and nutmeg. Bake, uncovered, at 350° for 60-70 minutes or until apples are tender. **Yield:** 6 servings.

GOLDEN FRUIT COCKTAIL

Jenny Hughson, Mitchell, Nebraska

My family and friends love the combination of the many fruits and fruit juices in this sweet hot fruit cocktail. It especially warms you up on cold winter days.

    3/4 cup packed brown sugar
    1/3 cup orange juice
    1/4 cup butter *or* margarine
    2 tablespoons lemon juice
    1 tablespoon cornstarch
    2 teaspoons grated orange peel
    1 cup sliced peaches
    1 cup sliced pears
    1 cup pineapple chunks
    1 cup mandarin orange segments
    12 maraschino cherries

In a large saucepan, combine brown sugar, orange juice, butter, lemon juice, cornstarch and orange peel. Cook and stir until mixture boils; cook 2 more minutes. Add remaining ingredients; heat through. **Yield:** 6-8 servings.

HEARTY FRUIT COMPOTE

Mary Margarett Coble, Edna, Kansas

This compote is packed with so many kinds of fruit it's almost a meal in itself!

    1 cup apple juice
    1 cinnamon stick (2 inches)
    1/2 cup coarsely chopped dried pitted prunes
    1/2 cup coarsely chopped dried apricots
    1 tablespoon grated orange peel
    1 medium orange, peeled, sectioned and
      chopped
    1 medium grapefruit, peeled, sectioned and
      chopped
    1 medium Granny Smith apple, peeled and
      chopped
    1 firm banana, sliced
    1/3 cup orange juice
    2 tablespoons brown sugar
    3 tablespoons chopped walnuts

In a saucepan, cook and stir apple juice and cinnamon stick until mixture boils. Remove from the heat; add prunes and apricots. Cover and let stand for 6 hours or overnight or until fruit is soft. Remove cinnamon stick. Add orange peel, orange, grapefruit, apple, banana, orange juice and brown sugar; mix well. Pour into serving bowl. Top with walnuts. **Yield:** 4-6 servings.

PEACHY YOGURT SHAKE

Charity Lovelace, Anchorage, Alaska

Here's a unique way to eat fruit for breakfast. My two preschoolers think they're really getting away with something when I serve these "milk shakes".

> 3/4 cup milk
> 2 cups sliced peaches
> 1 cup peach-flavored yogurt
> 1 cup cracked ice
> 2 tablespoons sugar
> 2 drops almond extract

In a blender container, place all ingredients in the order indicated. Process until smooth. **Yield:** 3-4 servings.

EASY MINT HOT CHOCOLATE

Sue Fisher, Northfield Falls, Vermont

This quick and easy beverage is perfect to serve the family on winter mornings before they head out into the cold. You'll love the tasty minty flavor.

> 6 Andes chocolate mints
> 16 ounces chocolate milk
> Mini marshmallows, optional

In a small saucepan, melt the mints over low heat. Slowly whisk in chocolate milk until well blended; heat but do not boil. Pour into mugs; top with mini marshmallows if desired. **Yield:** 2 servings.

SCRUMPTIOUS BREAKFAST FRUIT SOUP

Muriel Donaldson, Pasadena, California

About 25 years ago, I received this recipe from my husband's aunt, whose grandmother often prepared it in Denmark. Now it's one of the most requested dishes in my own family.

> 6 cups water
> 4 tablespoons quick-cooking tapioca
> 1 cinnamon stick (2 inches)
> 1 can (29 ounces) sliced peaches with syrup
> 2-1/2 cups assorted dried fruits, chopped
> 1 cup pitted prunes
> 1 cup raisins
> Juice of 1 lemon

In a large heavy saucepan, bring water, tapioca and cinnamon stick to a boil; reduce heat and simmer, stirring frequently, for 15 minutes or until tapioca begins to thicken. Add remaining ingredients and continue to cook on medium heat for 15 minutes, stirring frequently. Remove from the heat; cover and let stand for 30 minutes. Remove cinnamon stick. Fruit will continue to plump. Serve warm or cold. **Yield:** 8-10 servings.

YOGURT HONEY FRUIT BOWL

Margaret Matzke, Good Thunder, Minnesota

On our farm, husband Loren and I have visitors year-round. We enjoy sharing this delicious and nutritious dish with friends and family at breakfast.

> 3/4 teaspoon cornstarch
> 1/8 teaspoon salt
> 1/4 cup honey
> 4 teaspoons lemon juice
> 1 egg yolk, lightly beaten
> 1 carton (8 ounces) plain yogurt
> 1 carton (8 ounces) frozen whipped topping, thawed
> 4 cups chopped mixed fresh fruit
> 1/2 cup chopped nuts
> 1/2 cup granola

In a small saucepan, combine cornstarch and salt. Blend in honey and lemon juice; cook over medium-low heat, stirring constantly until thickened and bubbly. Cook and stir another 2 minutes. Gradually stir half of the hot mixture into the egg yolk; return all to the saucepan and cook for 2 minutes. Remove from the heat; blend in yogurt. Cool completely. Fold in whipped topping. Layer a fourth of the fruit, yogurt mixture, nuts and granola in a serving bowl. Repeat layers, ending with granola. Refrigerate. **Yield:** 6-8 servings.

MAKE-AHEAD RHUBARB SLUSH

Lorenda Glade, Ocheyedan, Iowa

If you're blessed with an abundance of rhubarb each spring, this recipe is for you! Whether you use fresh or frozen rhubarb, it's a refreshing accompaniment for any brunch.

> 8 cups sliced fresh *or* frozen rhubarb
> 2 quarts water
> 3 cups sugar
> 1/2 cup lemon juice
> 1 package (3 ounces) strawberry-flavored gelatin
> Lemon-lime soda, optional

In a Dutch oven or large kettle, combine rhubarb, water, sugar and lemon juice; cook until the rhubarb is tender. Strain, reserving juice. Add gelatin to hot juice, stirring until dissolved. Pour into a 5-qt. container or individual plastic cups; freeze. To serve, allow mixture to thaw until slushy. If desired, add 2 tablespoons lemon-lime soda to each serving. **Yield:** 12 servings.

Cookin' Up...
BREAKFASTS FOR KIDS

With these fun and flavorful recipes, your kids will run to the breakfast table instead of out the door! Most are easy enough for them to help prepare, too!

EASY ORANGE ROLLS

Peggy Kraemer, Thief River Falls, Minnesota
(PICTURED AT LEFT)

Life on a dairy farm is busy, so I need breakfast recipes that are simple yet delicious. My teenage daughter has been helping in the kitchen for years. In fact, this was probably one of the first recipes she made herself.

  1 cup sugar
1/2 cup butter *or* margarine
1/4 cup orange juice
  2 tablespoons grated orange peel
  3 tubes (10 ounces *each*) refrigerated biscuits

In a saucepan, combine sugar, butter, orange juice and peel. Heat until sugar is dissolved and butter is melted. Pour into a greased 10-in. fluted tube pan. Place 12 biscuits on their sides in a ring around the outer edge, overlapping slightly. Arrange remaining biscuits in the same manner, creating two more rings (one of 10 biscuits and one of eight). Bake at 350° for 25-30 minutes or until golden brown. Immediately turn upside down onto serving platter. Serve warm. **Yield:** 12-16 servings.

NESTLED EGG MUFFINS

Sharon Voth, Alexander, Manitoba
(PICTURED AT LEFT)

My kids think these muffins are great because the eggs "magically" cook in the shell as they rest on top of the muffin. For extra fun, we dye the eggs before baking.

  2 cups whole wheat flour
  2 cups old-fashioned oats
1/2 cup sugar
  2 tablespoons baking powder
1-1/2 teaspoons salt
  2 eggs, lightly beaten
1-1/2 cups milk
  1 cup raisins
3/4 cup vegetable oil
  18 whole uncooked eggs, rinsed

KIDDING AROUND. *Pictured at left, top to bottom: Easy Orange Rolls, Nestled Egg Muffins and Funny Face Toast (all recipes on this page).*

In a large bowl, combine flour, oats, sugar, baking powder and salt; set aside. Combine eggs, milk, raisins and oil; mix well. Stir into dry ingredients just until moistened. Fill 18 greased or paper-lined muffin cups half full. Place one whole egg (with shell) on top of each muffin. Bake at 400° for 18-20 minutes. Cut an egg open to test for desired doneness. Serve warm. **Yield:** 1-1/2 dozen. **Editor's Note:** Uncooked eggs may be dyed with food coloring before being placed in the muffins.

FUNNY FACE TOAST

Mary Kay Morris, Cokato, Minnesota
(PICTURED AT LEFT)

My two young boys are enthusiastic about learning to cook. So whenever I head for the kitchen, they volunteer to measure, scoop, pour and stir. And with this fun breakfast idea, they also practice their "painting"... without ruining my walls!

  1 tablespoon milk for each color desired
  3 to 4 drops food coloring of any colors desired
Bread

In a small bowl, combine milk and food coloring. With a small spoon, cotton swabs or clean small paintbrush, "paint" a face on a piece of bread. Toast as usual.

CINNAMON-MARSHMALLOW SURPRISES

Juli Ellis, Lees Summit, Missouri

These muffins are a surprise because no one can guess what makes them so good and gooey. Around our house they disappear quickly, so I often make a double batch.

  3 tablespoons sugar
  1 teaspoon ground cinnamon
  1 tube (10 ounces) refrigerated biscuits
  10 large marshmallows
1/4 cup butter *or* margarine, melted

Combine sugar and cinnamon; set aside. Flatten biscuits. Roll marshmallows in butter and then in cinnamon-sugar. Place one marshmallow on top of each biscuit; wrap biscuits around marshmallows and pinch seams. Place seam side down in greased muffin cups. Bake at 350° for 15-20 minutes or until golden brown. **Yield:** 10 servings.

TOAD IN THE HOLE

Ruth Lechleiter, Breckenridge, Minnesota

This is one of the first recipes I had my children pre-pare when they were learning to cook. My "little ones" are now grown (and have advanced to more difficult recipes!), but this continues to be a traditional standby in my home and theirs.

    1 slice of bread
    1 teaspoon butter *or* margarine
    1 egg
Salt and pepper to taste

Cut a 3-in. hole in the middle of the bread and discard. In a small skillet, melt the butter; place the bread in the skillet. Place egg in the hole. Cook for about 2 minutes over medium heat until the bread is lightly browned. Turn and cook the other side until egg reaches desired doneness. Season with salt and pepper. **Yield:** 1 serving.

BREAKFAST BUNDLES

Bernice Williams, North Aurora, Illinois

Getting kids to eat breakfast is a breeze when you offer them these little bundles of goodness packed with hearty ingredients. The recipe is simple so kids of all ages can help make them.

    1/2 cup butter *or* margarine, softened
    2 tablespoons orange juice concentrate
    1 egg, lightly beaten
1-1/2 cups all-purpose flour
    2/3 cup sugar
    1/2 cup Grape-Nuts cereal
    1 teaspoon baking powder
    1/2 pound sliced bacon, cooked and crumbled

In a mixing bowl, beat butter and orange juice. Add egg; mix well. Combine flour, sugar, cereal and baking powder; stir into butter mixture. Fold in bacon. Drop by rounded teaspoonfuls onto ungreased cookie sheets. Bake at 350° for 11-13 minutes or until edges are lightly brown. Store in the refrigerator. **Yield:** 2 dozen.

PIGS IN A BLANKET

Sue Krisher, Hermosa, South Dakota

This pancake and sausage combination is great to make for a slumber party breakfast. Kids will have fun eating their way to the tasty "pig" hiding in the golden pancake blanket.

    2 cups all-purpose flour
    1 teaspoon baking soda
    1 teaspoon baking powder
    1 teaspoon salt
    2 eggs, lightly beaten
2-1/4 cups buttermilk

    1/4 cup vegetable oil
    16 to 18 pork sausage links, cooked
SYRUP:
    1 cup sugar
    1 cup packed dark brown sugar
    1/2 cup water
    1/2 teaspoon vanilla extract
    1/2 teaspoon maple flavoring

In a mixing bowl, combine flour, baking soda, baking powder and salt. Combine eggs, buttermilk and oil; blend into dry ingredients. Pour batter by 1/4 cupfuls onto a lightly greased hot griddle; turn when bubbles form on top of pancakes. Cook until the second side is golden brown. Roll each pancake around a sausage link. For syrup, bring sugars and water to a boil. Stir in flavorings. Serve warm over pancakes. **Yield:** 16-18 pancakes (1-1/2 cups syrup).

STRAWBERRY-STUFFED FRENCH TOAST

Julie Vogl, Cumberland, Iowa

This simple stuffed French toast is great to serve the family for weekend breakfasts. The sweet creamy filling is sure to satisfy anyone's sweet tooth.

    1 package (3 ounces) cream cheese, softened
    1/2 cup strawberry yogurt
1-1/2 teaspoons vanilla extract, *divided*
    8 slices of white bread
    4 eggs
    1/4 cup milk
    1 tablespoon butter *or* margarine
    1 cup sliced fresh strawberries, sweetened to taste

In a small mixing bowl, mix cream cheese, yogurt and 1/2 teaspoon vanilla until smooth. Spread 2 tablespoons on four slices of bread; top with remaining bread to make four sandwiches. Beat eggs, milk and remaining vanilla; dip sandwiches. In a skillet, melt butter. Fry sandwiches until golden brown on both sides. To serve, top each sandwich with 1 tablespoon cream cheese mixture and 1/4 cup strawberries. **Yield:** 4 servings.

SIX-WEEK BRAN MUFFINS

Michele Garber, East Petersburg, Pennsylvania

I'm only 12 years old but already like to cook and bake. This batter can be made ahead and stored in the refrigerator for weeks, so it's easy to make yummy muffins fresh each morning.

    4 eggs
    3 cups sugar
    1 quart buttermilk
    6 cups bran cereal with raisins
    5 cups all-purpose flour
    1 cup vegetable oil
    5 teaspoons baking soda
    1 teaspoon salt

In a large bowl, beat eggs and sugar until well combined. Stir in buttermilk, cereal, flour, oil, baking soda and salt; mix well. Refrigerate at least 6 hours before using. Fill greased or paper-lined muffin cups two-thirds full. Bake at 400° for 15-20 minutes or until a toothpick inserted near the center comes out clean. Batter may be stored, covered, in the refrigerator for up to 6 weeks. **Yield:** 5-6 dozen.

PEANUT BUTTER 'N' JELLY BREAKFAST SHAKE
Loretta Levitz, Allston, Massachusetts

My husband is a big "kid" who'll often whip up this tasty shake for breakfast on the go. Your kids will love the flavor of a peanut butter and jelly sandwich in it.

> 2 cups milk
> 1 ripe banana, sliced
> 2 tablespoons peanut butter
> 2 tablespoons jam, jelly *or* preserves (any flavor)
> 1/2 teaspoon vanilla extract

Place all of the ingredients in a blender; blend for 3 minutes or until smooth. Serve cold. **Yield:** 1-2 servings (2-1/2 cups).

HAM AND CHEESE WAFFLES
Doris Wright, Graham, Washington

Like most kids, my children love pizza...given the chance, they'd probably eat it for every meal! So their eyes lit up when I first served these waffles with pizza-like ingredients for breakfast.

> 3 eggs
> 2 cups milk
> 1/3 cup vegetable oil
> 2-1/2 cups all-purpose flour
> 2 teaspoons baking powder
> 1/2 teaspoon salt
> 1-1/2 cups (6 ounces) shredded mozzarella cheese
> 1/2 to 3/4 cup cubed fully cooked ham *or* Canadian bacon
> Fried eggs, optional

In a bowl, beat eggs, milk and oil. Combine flour, baking powder and salt; add to egg mixture and beat until smooth. Fold in cheese and ham or bacon. Bake in a waffle iron according to manufacturer's directions until golden brown. Top each waffle with a fried egg if desired. **Yield:** 8-10 waffles (6-1/2 inches).

SWEET SUBSTITUTION. *Vary the flavor of French toast by using cinnamon raisin bread instead of plain white bread. Your kids will love it!*

SCRAMBLED FRENCH TOAST
Torrey Stuart, Eugene, Oregon

I make a point of saving my leftover bread just so I can make this family-favorite recipe. Kids will have fun helping you prepare it, but will enjoy eating this sticky "scrambled" version of French toast even more!

> 4 eggs
> 2 cups milk
> 2 teaspoons vanilla extract
> 1 teaspoon ground cinnamon
> 1/2 teaspoon ground nutmeg
> 12 cups cubed day-old bread (1/2-inch cubes)
> 3 tablespoons butter *or* margarine
> 1/2 to 2/3 cup sugar

In a large bowl, beat eggs. Add milk, vanilla, cinnamon and nutmeg. Add bread cubes and toss; let stand for 5 minutes. Melt butter in a large skillet. Add bread cubes and stir until cooked and browned. Gradually add sugar; stir to coat evenly. Cook until all sugar is dissolved, about 5 minutes. **Yield:** 6-8 servings.

SAUSAGE BALLS
Dinah Overlien, Jim Falls, Wisconsin

These are a fun variation from regular sausage links or patties. Have the kids help shape them into balls, then serve with eggs, pancakes or any other breakfast item.

> 1 pound bulk pork sausage
> 3 cups buttermilk biscuit mix
> 3 cups (12 ounces) shredded sharp cheddar cheese
> 2 eggs, lightly beaten

In a bowl, combine all ingredients. Shape into 1-in. balls and place on a rack in a shallow baking pan. Bake at 375° for 25-30 minutes or until golden brown. Or freeze and bake frozen at 425° for 15-20 minutes or until golden brown. **Yield:** 3 dozen.

BUTTERSCOTCH TOAST
Gerry Rice, Greenville, Michigan

I first started using this recipe about 40 years ago when our kids were little. They were always delighted when this showed up on the breakfast table. And I was delighted that they were taking time to eat breakfast!

> 1/4 cup packed brown sugar
> 3 tablespoons butter *or* margarine, softened
> 1 teaspoon light cream
> 6 to 8 pieces of toast

In a mixing bowl, beat brown sugar, butter and cream until smooth. Spread on toast. Broil 4 in. from the heat for 1-2 minutes or until bubbly. **Yield:** 6-8 servings.

🫖🫖🫖 INDEX 🫖🫖🫖

Cheesy Herbed Eggs, 27
Ham 'n' Cheese Strata, 6
Ham and Cheese Biscuits, 23
Ham and Cheese Waffles, 93
Home-Style Cheese Muffins, 77

CHERRIES
Cheery Cherry Bread, 60
Cherry-Raspberry Jam, 61

CHOCOLATE
Chocolate Cinnamon Buns, 60
Chocolate-Oat Granola, 82
Cocoa Cinnamon Spread, 56
Easy Mint Hot Chocolate, 89
Hot Cocoa Mix, 88

COFFEE CAKES, DANISH & SWEET ROLLS
Apricot Coffee Cake, 54
Blueberry Breakfast Cake, 55
Breakfast Nut Roll, 64
Buttermilk Coffee Cake, 67
Chocolate Cinnamon Buns, 60
Cinnamon-Marshmallow
    Surprises, 91
Cranberry Coffee Cake, 51
Danish Kringle, 54
Easy Orange Rolls, 91
Graham-Streusel Coffee Cake, 51
Heart-Shaped Coffee Cake, 59
Holiday Sour Cream Rings, 63
Lemon Kolaches, 54
Luscious Lemon Coffee Cake, 58
Nutty Lemon Coffee Cake, 61
Orange Coffee Cake, 58
Overnight Berry Coffee Cake, 60
Pear Cake with Sour Cream
    Topping, 58
Prune-Filled Danish, 64
Pull-Apart Morning Rolls, 58
Raspberry Coffee Cake, 67
Sticky Cinnamon Rolls, 55
Swiss Butterhorns, 63

CORNMEAL
Blueberry Cornmeal Muffins, 75
Cornmeal Hotcakes, 40
Fried Cornmeal Mush, 28

CRANBERRIES
Apple-Filled Cranberry Muffins, 77
Cranberry Coffee Cake, 51
Cranberry Orange Loaf, 63
Cranberry Yogurt Muffins, 77
Cranberry-Cardamom Muffins, 76
Hot Cranberry Drink, 86

DATES
Mixed Grain and Wild Rice
    Cereal, 83
Orange Muffins with Dates, 77
Spiced Date Oatmeal, 81

DOUGHNUTS
Banana Fritters, 61
Cider Doughnuts, 67
Pennsylvania Dutch Potato
    Doughnuts, 50
Snowflake Doughnuts, 55

EGG DISHES
(See Casseroles; Omelets; Quiches; and Scrambled Eggs)

FRENCH TOAST
Apple-Cinnamon Baked French
    Toast, 42
Baked French Toast with
    Home-Style Syrup, 41
Banana-Stuffed French Toast, 47
Blueberry French Toast Cobbler, 43
Cheddar French Toast with Dried
    Fruit Syrup, 45
Eggnog French Toast, 43
Freezer French Toast, 45
French Toast Supreme, 35
Honey-Baked French Toast, 37
Orange French Toast, 42
Overnight Caramel French Toast, 46
Scrambled French Toast, 93
Strawberry-Banana French Toast, 40
Strawberry-Stuffed French Toast, 92
Stuffed French Toast with Berry
    Sauce, 46

FRUIT DISHES
Cinnamon-Honey Grapefruit, 86
Golden Fruit Cocktail, 88
Hearty Fruit Compote, 88
Mandarin Orange Salad, 86
Mary's Baked Fruit, 85
Orange-Pecan Baked Apples, 88
Overnight Fruit Cup, 85
Scrumptious Breakfast Fruit
    Soup, 89
Slush Fruit Cups, 86
Spiced Pears, 85
Yogurt Honey Fruit Bowl, 89

GRAVIES & SAUCES
Country Sausage Gravy, 30
Creamed Ham and Eggs, 30
New Orleans Brunch Eggs, 31
Quick Sausage Gravy, 25
Southern Eggs and Biscuits, 13

GRITS & HOMINY
Fried Sausage Grits, 33
Golden Country Grits, 15
Home-Style Hominy Casserole, 18

Overnight Sausage and Grits, 18

HAM
Brunch Enchiladas, 16
Creamed Ham and Eggs, 30
Farmhouse Omelet, 5
Ham 'n' Cheese Strata, 6
Ham and Cheese Biscuits, 23
Ham and Cheese Waffles, 93
Ham and Potato Casserole, 19
Hearty Ham Omelet, 25
Italian Breakfast Casseroles, 15
New Orleans Brunch Eggs, 31
Pleasing Potato Pie, 6
Rice-Crust Quiche, 7
Southwest Skillet Dish, 31

HONEY
Cinnamon-Honey Grapefruit, 86
Cornflake Waffles with Honey
    Sauce, 47
Honey Apple Topping, 42
Honey-Baked French Toast, 37
Honey Cereal Bites, 82
Honey Coconut Granola, 80
Honey Granola Bread, 59
Honey Nut Topping, 43
Pancakes with Orange Honey
    Butter, 45
Peanut Butter-Honey Bars, 83
Yogurt Honey Fruit Bowl, 89

JAMS & MARMALADES
Apple Pie Jam, 56
Blushing Peach Jam, 56
Caramel Apple Jam, 50
Cherry-Raspberry Jam, 61
Cinnamon Plum Jam, 56
Easy Lemon-Blueberry Jam, 51
Rhubarb Raisin Marmalade, 51
Strawberry-Rhubarb Jam, 58

LEMON
Easy Lemon-Blueberry Jam, 51
Lemon Curd, 50
Lemon Kolaches, 54
Lemon Poppy Seed Bread, 49
Lemon/Raspberry Streusel
    Muffins, 75
Low-Fat Lemon Poppy Seed
    Muffins, 73
Luscious Lemon Coffee Cake, 58
Nutty Lemon Coffee Cake, 61

MUFFINS
Apple-Filled Cranberry Muffins, 77
Banana Praline Muffins, 72
Blueberry Cornmeal Muffins, 75
Breakfast in a Muffin, 71
Cinnamon-Topped Rhubarb
    Muffins, 73
Cranberry Yogurt Muffins, 77
Cranberry-Cardamom Muffins, 76
Early-Riser Muffins, 73
Easy Oat Bran Muffins, 76

Sausage Quiche, 10
Savory Spinach Pie, 11
Slumber Party Pie, 19
Wild Rice Quiche, 16
Zucchini Brunch Pie, 13

Egg and Sausage Pockets, 27
Hot Jam Breakfast Sandwiches, 31
Sausage Swirls, 13
Stuffed Breakfast Loaf, 20
Wake-Up Sandwiches, 22

Strawberry-Banana French Toast, 40
Strawberry-Rhubarb Jam, 58
Strawberry-Stuffed French Toast, 92

QUICK BREADS
Banana Nut Bread, 68
Blueberry Brunch Loaf, 65
Blueberry Quick Bread, 69
Cheery Cherry Bread, 60
Cranberry Orange Loaf, 63
Crunchy Apple Bread, 69
Lemon Poppy Seed Bread, 49
Pumpkin Bread, 64
Spiced Rhubarb Bread, 65
Strawberry Bread, 61
Sweet Potato Bread, 68
Thanksgiving Bread, 65
Zucchini Snack Bread, 65

RASPBERRIES
Cherry-Raspberry Jam, 61
Lemon/Raspberry Streusel
    Muffins, 75
Overnight Berry Coffee Cake, 60
Raspberry Coffee Cake, 67

RHUBARB
Cinnamon-Topped Rhubarb
    Muffins, 73
Make-Ahead Rhubarb Slush, 89
Rhubarb Raisin Marmalade, 51
Spiced Rhubarb Bread, 65
Strawberry-Rhubarb Jam, 58

RICE
Egg Foo Yung Breakfast, 33
Mixed Grain and Wild Rice
    Cereal, 83
Rice-Crust Quiche, 7
Spanish-Style Breakfast Bake, 14
Wild Rice Quiche, 16

SANDWICHES
Bacon-Potato Burritos, 31
Breakfast Burritos, 27
Brunch Tidbits, 22
Canadian Bacon Breakfast, 30

SAUSAGE
Applesauce/Sausage Waffles, 36
Breakfast Pizza, 6
Christmas Morning Pie, 18
Country Sausage Gravy, 30
Egg and Sausage Pockets, 27
Fried Sausage Grits, 33
Hearty Egg Casserole, 16
Hearty Sausage Loaf, 59
Home-Style Hominy Casserole, 18
Italian Sausage Casserole, 10
Lazy Day Casserole, 7
Overnight Sausage and Grits, 18
Pigs in a Blanket, 92
Pork Sausage Ring, 5
Quick Sausage Gravy, 25
Sausage Balls, 93
Sausage Quiche, 10
Sausage Strata, 23
Sausage Swirls, 13
Skier's Skillet, 33
Slumber Party Pie, 19
Spicy Breakfast Lasagna, 6
Spicy Sausage Casserole, 22
Stuffed Breakfast Loaf, 20
Wild Rice Quiche, 16

SCRAMBLED EGGS
All-in-One-Casserole, 14
Bacon-Potato Burritos, 31
Breakfast Burritos, 27
Breakfast Mess, 33
Cheesy Herbed Eggs, 27
Curried Scrambled Egg, 25
Egg and Sausage Pockets, 27
Farmer's Country Breakfast, 26
Fast and Flavorful Eggs, 28
Garden Fresh Breakfast, 30
Make-Ahead Scrambled Eggs, 11
One-Pan Breakfast, 28
Pork Sausage Ring, 5
Salmon Scramble, 26
South-of-the-Border Scrambled
    Eggs, 26
Vegetable Scrambled Eggs, 25

SEAFOOD
Easter Stuffed Eggs, 14
Salmon Scramble, 26

STRAWBERRIES
Strawberry Bread, 61
Strawberry Streusel Muffins, 73

SYRUPS & TOPPINGS
Apple-Cinnamon Syrup, 46
Blueberry Syrup, 43
Fresh Peach Sauce, 46
Honey Apple Topping, 42
Honey Nut Topping, 43

TOAST
Butterscotch Toast, 93
Funny Face Toast, 91

WAFFLES
Applesauce/Sausage Waffles, 36
Bacon Waffles, 37
Buttermilk Waffles, 45
Cornflake Waffles with Honey
    Sauce, 47
Gingerbread Waffles, 47
Ham and Cheese Waffles, 93
Oatmeal Nut Waffles, 40
Potato Waffles, 43
Quick and Easy Waffles, 42
Traditional Waffles, 46
Waffles with Vanilla Sauce, 35
World's Best Waffles, 37

YEAST BREADS
Cream Cheese Bread, 60
English Muffin Bread, 56
Hearty Sausage Loaf, 59
Honey Granola Bread, 59
Whole Wheat Toasting Bread, 49
Wonderful English Muffins, 49

ZUCCHINI
Garden Fresh Breakfast, 30
Zucchini Brunch Pie, 13
Zucchini Omelet, 14
Zucchini Potato Pancakes, 36
Zucchini Snack Bread, 65

TO ORDER additional copies of *Cookin' Up Country Breakfasts*, send $9.98 each plus $2.50 shipping/handling to Country Store, Suite **3361**, P.O. Box 990, Greendale WI 53129. Please specify item number **19549**. Credit card orders call toll free **1-800/558-1013**.

Looking for More Country Cooking at Its Down-Home Best?

Our other popular cookbooks are sure to satisfy!

Country Ground Beef. If you're always looking for hearty ways to serve the country's favorite meat, look no further! This 100-page cookbook is *stuffed* with some 300 *never-before-published recipes* that are big on taste, short on effort and economical besides. You'll win praise with *delicious* skillet suppers...main-dish soups...oven meals...plus sandwiches, meat pies and more. Many of the dishes are shown in *full color* so you can see what they'll look like. And each recipe has won raves from the families of the country cooks who share them with you. With so many new ways to use ground beef, you'll reach for this practical cookbook often!

11608 Country Ground Beef...**$9.98**

Bountiful Harvest. Put the goodies from your garden—or the local produce department—to hundreds of delicious *new* uses with this unique 100-page cookbook! Every chapter "stars" a different country-fresh fruit or vegetable in dozens of mouth-watering *main dishes*...tempting side dishes and salads...plus soups, sandwiches and even delectable desserts. *Bountiful Harvest* gives you some *300* lip-smacking ideas for just about every morsel of homegrown goodness you're likely to grow or buy, from asparagus to zucchini. Each recipe comes from a great country cook...and many dishes are even shown in full-color photos, so you can *see* them even before you head to your garden. You'll find many *mmm-good* ideas for country-fresh produce in this one-of-a-kind book.

18536 Bountiful Harvest...**$9.98**

Grandma's Great Desserts. Treat your family to the kind of hearty old-fashioned desserts Grandma used to serve up. This photo-packed, easy-to-use cookbook is bursting with some 300 heirloom family recipes for crisp cobblers laced with cinnamon...oven-warm pies with the flakiest crusts...even Quick & Easy selections that only *taste* as though they took hours to prepare! You'll discover "secret" hints to help you bake your best and "hear" the heartwarming stories behind these treats as well.

7429 Grandma's Great Desserts...**$10.98**

The Best of Country Cooking. Nothing says "country" like good hearty cooking—so what could be better than a GIANT treasury busting with the *best* country cooking ever? *This is it...*our biggest-ever cookbook, with *more than 750* of the best family-pleasing recipes ever to appear in any of our Reiman Publications magazines and in our *A Taste of the Country* cookbook series. That's almost *triple* the size of any cookbook we've ever published before—and *more than 500 dishes* are pictured in full color to tempt your taste buds even before you start cooking. Plus, we've given this 290-page cookbook a durable *hard cover* with a concealed spiral binding, so you can depend on it for *years* to come!

11742 The Best of Country Cooking...**$24.98**

TO ORDER: Send check or money order plus $2.50 shipping and handling for each book ordered. Please specify books by item number. Send to Country Store, Suite 3380, P.O. Box 990, Greendale WI 53129. Credit card orders call toll-free **1-800/558-1013**.